The Secrets
Behind the Eyes
Life (?) After Abortion

Valley Walker Press, New Plymouth, Idaho

JoEllen Claypool

Copyright 2013 by JoEllen Claypool
Published by Valley Walker Press
New Plymouth, ID 83655

Cover designed by Thom Hollis
Edited by Deborah Archer and Sheila F. Eismann

For more information or additional copies please contact:
Valley Walker Press
P.O. Box 288
New Plymouth, ID 83655
valleywalkerpress@hotmail.com

First printing 2013

ISBN – 978-0-9857658-2-8
Library of Congress Control Number   2013951089

Dedication

I want to dedicate this book to the Healing Hearts Team at the Hope Pregnancy Center in Ontario, Oregon and to each woman who desires to be healed from her past.

Acknowledgements

I am so thankful for the women who were bold enough to be transparent about their experiences which gave me the courage to reach out for healing. The Healing Hearts leaders were my angels as they led me to the truth, helping me cross each painful hurdle.

My gratitude for my husband can hardly be expressed in words. His strength and commitment to me during my tough times only made me love him more. He supported me emotionally as I came face to face with my past. He went above and beyond with his patience and understanding.

Appreciation goes out to my family and friends for their understanding as I shared my story. Instead of judging, they wrapped me in their love and encouraged me during my "down times." They showered me with verses from God's Word to remind me of His love for me.

I was so thankful for Dallas and Danny being willing to be transparent and share their input from a man's perspective. We can't forget about the men who have had their lives altered, as well, regarding this issue.

I am grateful to Debi Archer for being so willing to write my foreword and help with editing when the opportunity presented itself. She has such a beautiful heart to be used by God and serve wherever she happens to be. She has been a great example to me in the balance of boldness and meekness and being available in any aspect that God requests.

A huge thank you also goes out to my other editor, Sheila Eismann. Her thoroughness and guidance gave me a clear direction. She encouraged me regarding the timeliness of this topic.

I appreciate my cover designer, Thom Hollis, and his heart to help new authors on their exciting adventures. He really captured the images in my mind and from my heart.

CONTENTS

FOREWORD

2 Corinthians 5:21 "He made Him Who knew no sin to be sin for us that we might become the righteousness of God in Him." God came down from His glory in heaven to take on human flesh and be tempted in every way that we are tempted. He never sinned, not even a little "white" lie!

The penalty of eternal destruction was mine for my sin. Jesus went to the cross, suffered, bled and died in my place. He exchanged my filthy, sin-filled life for His perfect, holy life. When God sees me, He sees me as being perfect, as if I had NEVER sinned because of the exchanged life that I have by faith in Christ. That is why I cannot stop "ReJoySing!" O for God's amazing grace, I am eternally grateful!

All sin is the same in the eyes of the Lord from loving something or someone more than we love God (idolatry), to half-truths (lying) , to murder (in my case abortion). The death inflicted, by me, upon my dear little girl, Lindsay, who would have been born around June 8, 1984, caused my grief-laden rivers of tears to gush as nothing else had in my life.

On March 10, 1985, I was born-again by the Holy Spirit. My eyes were opened to my sin. My Godly sorrow would later lead me to true repentance. By the amazing providence of God, He miraculously and personally orchestrated all of the details for me to be forgiven by Him and set free from my abortion. All glory to God!

Today, I realize that my abortion was not in vain. God has given me a transparent life for Him to show others His forgiveness, restoration, and loving kindness in order for Him to encourage others of the hope for them in Jesus.

My prayer for you is that God will reach deep down into the innermost being of your heart as He uses JoEllen in her book, *The Secrets Behind the Eyes*, as one of His instruments to show *you* His amazing grace, loving counsel and guidance. May you hear the voice of the Lover of your soul, the Lord Jesus Christ, as the Holy Spirit encourages you, teaches you, admonishes, comforts, reproves and trains you in righteousness by His Word, the Holy Bible.

One of my favorite passages in the entire Bible is Jesus' prayer to the Father for us in the whole chapter of John 17. It is well worth our time and attention to tarry often there. John 17:17 "Sanctify them (purify, consecrate, separate them for Yourself, make them holy) by Truth, Your Word is Truth." May He lovingly draw you close, yes, closer still, to Himself as you surrender all to Jesus. Grace to you.

Debi

INTRODUCTION

There are so many worthy causes in the world that people can support. The situations that we experience in life help to develop our passion for certain areas of outreach. The key is to have the boldness to reach out.

Each person has a different story to share that can benefit others. It's important to bind together to help people heal from past hurts and to bring understanding to others regarding decisions and situations.

One piece of advice I have been given is to "write what you know." That is so much easier said than done. Some of the things we *know* are not pleasant. It takes a lot of courage to admit what you *know* and the experiences you have been through. This leaves you with a choice. You can remain silent or you can find your voice.

Remaining silent is safe. It is a comfort zone that protects us. We don't have to risk rejection and judgment. We can relax in our secure sanctuary of silence, but at what cost? As we are retreating, the world carries on. Turmoil continues in the lives of others. But our shield of silence surrounds us. We are protected.

Our other option is finding our voices. We have all survived something. We all have times in our past that have caused hurt. We were able to get through it though. Shouldn't we take the knowledge we have and share it with others? Why would we want to sit back and do nothing? Some of the information we have may help one person, but what if you possess wisdom that can change family trees?

It can be overwhelming thinking of the number of heartaches plaguing people today. How can one person make a difference? I think if we can break it down and not feel that we have to take on the whole world and its problems, we can accomplish something.

We need to start within our own sphere of influence. Start with your family and friends who might be dealing with something you know about. Consider the ministries in your church. If there is one that you can get involved in to help minister to others, do so. If you feel there is a need for another one that is not offered, start one yourself. Examine the needs of your community and get plugged in to help.

Healing can start with one person. YOU can make a difference. Be alert and listen as people talk. When we can be bold enough to share our stories, it can assure others that they are not alone. Be watchful of the people around you; their behavior and words can be a warning of distress happening in their lives. You can be the one to assure them that you see them and are concerned. It is very easy to feel invisible in this world.

I might be sounding pretty confident already. I will have you know that I have been working on this book for over a year and it has just been in the last month that I have admitted to only a handful of people the topic of this project. I would panic anytime I thought of this book being advertised. I am still concerned about announcing the finish of it in certain circles. I feel very vulnerable. Some people know my story but many do not.

One thing stands true though. I am tired of being quiet. It is exhausting. I started seeing opportunities for me to speak up. Regretfully, I did not take advantage of some of the first moments I had. I was able to see the damage caused by my silence. It broke my heart. You can bet the next time I was given the chance, I was fearless. I spoke up and didn't care of the judgment that might come my way. There were times I was able to be very adamant in disclosing the needed information. Other situations required a more gentle approach.

Doing the right thing is not always easy. There is sacrifice involved as well as risk. So what do you do? It comes down to this: the right thing is the right thing. Praying for strength and guidance can supply you with the confidence you will need. Finding somebody you can be transparent with that can join you in prayer is very helpful. You have to face the fact that you *do* have something to offer and you *can* make a difference.

The book has been put together in a way that I weave my own story into every other chapter with the alternate chapters sharing facts and statistics about abortion. At the back of the book I have provided space for your own words. You will see references throughout the book that prompted the headings for these sections.

There is a space for you to write your own Psalm. Another page provides you with an opportunity to write a letter to someone in your life that you need to forgive. Of course you do not have to send the letter, but you will be amazed in the healing that can take place in writing out your feelings as if you were to share it.

Having a testimony to share is helpful in letting others know how you can relate to them. You may have a couple of different testimonies. Various situations call for different events to be shared. You can write those out in the pages reserved for that topic. I also provided an area for you to list different Bible verses that have impacted you along with a spot for you to write down a life verse and why you chose that particular verse.

Take advantage of those pages so that you can see how you can be used in the lives of others. I am praying, in advance, for those of you who pick up this book. I know that eyes will be opened and hearts will be healed. Above all, I pray that you will find your voice and use it, with the full assurance that you will save lives!

1

NO VICTORY

One in four women **in the church** has had an abortion. Does that surprise you? What astonished me was that it didn't matter the size of the church; a church of four hundred people or a church of thirty. When I told my story, women would come out of the woodwork to share their own experiences.

My other question: why would it surprise us? We hear the staggering numbers of aborted babies. In the United States alone, 1.37 million abortions are performed each year averaging 4,000 each day. Worldwide, 42 million babies are killed yearly for an average 115,000 per day. Do we think it only happens in the cities? Do we think that only non-Christians are doing this? Are we so naïve to think, "Surely not people I know"?

Stop and think about it. Do we really take the time to get to know the people around us? Do we make the effort to get more than just acquainted with the people in our churches? Do we look into their eyes and try to get out of ourselves for one moment and see what they have seen? Do we even *want* to take the time to do that?

What is the basis of our fear? Are we afraid that they will tell us the truth if we create a safe place for them to open up? Are we concerned that we won't be equipped to handle the things they tell us? Are we worried it will take up too much of our precious time to help someone in need? Are we afraid that the person will have to be another one we cross off the friend or acquaintance list because they don't quite measure up to those with whom we choose to associate?

Now put the shoe on the other foot (because we all have our stories). Why don't we voluntarily offer information about our past? Why won't we let people really get to know us? Why won't we look people in the eye?

What makes us fearful? Are we worried about rejection? Are we concerned that people will judge us? Are we so naïve to think that we are the only ones who have lived these experiences? Are we afraid that we might have something to offer and that will take us too far out of our comfort zone?

Yes, one in four women in the church has had an abortion. How do you picture a woman who has gone through this: young, confused, women addicted to drugs or alcohol, promiscuous women, or callous, self-absorbed monsters? Do you see women like this sitting in your church?

Women who have made the choice to abort come from all walks of life and have different reasons for making the decision. Statistics show that as far as income is concerned,

28.7% account for the abortions performed on women who earn less than $15,000. The $15,000 to $29,999 bracket holds 19.5%. Another 38% are in the $30,000 to $59,999 category and 13.8% account for those earning more than $60,000.

Many arguments have stemmed from wanting abortion to be allowed for cases of rape or incest. Only 2% account for that reason though. Charts show that 48% admit that they didn't want to be a single parent or were having problems with their partner. Feeling unable to afford having a child was the reason of 73% and 74% said it was done for social reasons. They felt it would interfere with responsibilities they already had such as school or work.

Roe vs. Wade became the milestone of abortion becoming legal in the United States in 1973 at the Supreme Court level. This case dehumanized babies. It allowed that a fetus was part of the mother's body and not a separate body. Because of this, babies were not considered protected under the 14th amendment (namely that no person was allowed to be deprived of life, liberty or property without due process of law and no person could be denied equal protection of the laws). Therefore, a woman can give permission for an abortion as easy as giving permission to get a tattoo or any other alteration to her body.

By manipulating words, such as using fetus instead of baby, no one could really agree as to when life began. This helped in justifying abortions along with statements such as this one from a doctor: "Abortion has become right and ethical, as long as it is for the right reasons."

If fetuses are not separate bodies, why have hundreds of fetal surgeries been performed? If a baby is unwanted does that mean it is not a baby? One sign read, "If life ends when the heart stops beating, shouldn't life begin when the heart starts beating." A baby's heart begins beating at six weeks. "There is no period of unlife. All life comes from pre-existing life," one article stated.

The Bible says in **Genesis 1: 24-28 And God said, "Let the land produce living creatures according to their kinds: the livestock, the creatures that move along the ground, and the wild animals, each according to its kind." And it was so. God made the wild animals according to their kinds, the livestock according to their kinds, and all the creatures that move along the ground according to their kinds. And God saw that it was good.**

Then God said, "Let us make mankind in our image, in our likeness, so that they may rule over the fish in the sea and the birds in the sky, over the livestock and all the wild animals, and over all the creatures that move along the ground." So God created mankind in his own image, in the image of God he created them; male and female he created them. God blessed them and said to them, "Be fruitful and increase in number; fill the earth and subdue it. Rule over the fish in the sea and the birds in the sky and over every living creature that moves on the ground."

Also according to God's Word, the "fetus" is a separate being. It is a miracle of life. **Psalm 139:13-14 For you created my inmost being; you knit me together in my mother's womb. I praise you because I am fearfully and wonderfully made; your works are wonderful, I know that full well.**

Our society *claims* to regard human life as important. In fact, search and rescue authorities will go above and beyond searching for missing or injured people even past the point of assumed death, yet millions of humans are being grossly destroyed every year. We even go to great lengths to protect hundreds of endangered animals. Why don't human babies get the same protection?

The annual 42 million worldwide abortions averages out to seven times the amount of people killed in the Holocaust. We think of Hitler as a monster, yet we accept what is happening today. What amazes me is that this is being done in a first world country. Most of North America, Asia, Europe, Australia and India are the least restrictive in their abortion procedures. The most restrictive areas are in the third world countries.

To me, it seems a complete contradiction, especially after finding the following definitions of first world versus third world countries. A first world country is considered to have the highest standard of living, and most advanced technology. They are considered to be the greatest influences in the world. The term could also mean: industrialized nations, developed countries, rich countries or the civilized world. This stands in contrast to the poor, underdeveloped, uncivilized, exploited nations of the so called third world.

The words that stood out to me were "highest standard of living", "greatest influence", and "civilized world." I was confused, because these words didn't seem to match up with the numbers I was seeing on the charts. This led me to do a further word search. The words **standard, influence and civilized** all came up with descriptions of having a requirement of moral conduct and showing evidence of intellectual advancement. It also included the words humane, ethical, and reasonable. I guess the words that come to my mind when I see the astonishing numbers of abortions done daily are brutal, cruel, inhumane and merciless.

Before Roe vs. Wade, the issue of abortion was decided by each state. It had been illegal in 30 states and legal under certain conditions in 20 states. Before this case, the estimated number of illegal abortions during the time period of 1950 through 1960 was between 200,000 and 1.2 million.

During that time, anywhere from 160 to 260 women died each year from these unsafe procedures and thousands more were seriously injured. Today, abortion is one of the most commonly performed clinical procedures and the current death rate is less than 1 per 100,000. That almost looks like a reason to rejoice, doesn't it?

Late term abortions (procedures performed after the 20th gestational week) are becoming more prevalent today. I recently read, "There *are only* 500 to 600 late term abortions performed per year in the United States." ONLY?! That is 500 to 600 too many.

What these numbers do not relay, however, is the number of women who die emotionally daily because of the decision they made. It doesn't give a true understanding of the women who are tormented by memories, flashbacks and depression or the ones who are physically reminded on a daily basis of a choice of their past. Legalizing abortion and promoting the safer practices didn't make it any better or easier emotionally.

Roe vs. Wade was no victory. In fact, over 45 million babies have been murdered in the United States alone since that Supreme Court decision. Of those, 52% occurred in women under the age of 25 years old.

There is no victory in any aspect of this horrid practice. There is not one good thing that comes from it. Lives are lost. Minds are tormented. Hearts are infested with the diseases of resentment, bitterness, rage and unforgiveness. Relationships are destroyed. Family units are stunted. There is no victory.

2

WHAT'S WRONG WITH ME?

"I'm so sick," I moaned as I felt the soft, mauve recliner hot against my skin.

My mom walked past me with dust rag in hand, pausing to feel my forehead. I was 20 years old but I always loved that my mom would stop what she was doing to tend to my needs. Although I loved the attention from her, the rag soaked with cleaner solution sent me darting from the chair into the bathroom as everything that I had eaten that day revisited me.

Sweat moistened my forehead as I sobbed between heaves. When I was sure there was nothing more to come up, I sat with my back against the bathtub, my elbows resting on my bent knees, head in my hands. Mom was right there. She was always right there.

"This isn't right," she sympathized. "You need to see a doctor. There might be something really wrong. You have been sick every day for a while now."

"I will see how I am doing tomorrow and call if I need to," I said weakly as I moved past her to lie on the couch.

I was feeling better the next day although a bit tired. Performing my duties as a medical transcriptionist didn't require a lot of energy so I was able to work with no interruptions.

On the way home, I decided to stop for a taco. I purchased my usual chicken soft-shells and a small carton of milk. I ate them quickly as I had allowed myself to get too hungry and felt a bit queasy. I opened my milk and filled my mouth. I pulled the carton down quickly as my taste buds immediately understood the situation before me. The milk was sour!

There I was, sitting in a booth, in a room full of people and with my mouth full of sour milk. The only thing on my mind in that instant was wondering how I was gracefully going to get across the room without a bunch of stares and without tossing my tacos between my booth and the restroom. I moved as quickly, but as naturally, as I could praying the entire way that the tiny one room bathroom would not be locked and that it would be sound proof. With my prayer answered, I walked in and latched the top lock, turned around and let loose.

"I'm done," I thought. "Mom is right. I need to go in and figure out what is going on." Sour milk probably wouldn't have settled well with anybody, but I had a feeling there was more to it.

I called the doctor's office as soon as I got home. An appointment was made and, fortunately, I was able to get in that same week.

As I entered the clinic, I took a deep breath to prepare for the paperwork, the wait, the cup and whatever else was in store for me. The receptionist smiled warmly as she handed me the clipboard with the forms that would be added to my manila chart.

I filled out the address, phone and contact information and moved on to the family and personal medical history. There wasn't much to report. I had not had a whole lot of medical issues in the past. Yes, I do self breast exams, 0 for number of children and pregnancies; last menstrual cycle was almost two months ago. That was no cause for alarm. I had always been very irregular.

I took my completed paperwork to the desk and dutifully turned it in, grabbed a magazine and sat down to wait. I thumbed through it, not really paying attention to the words on the page. About 15 minutes passed before the nurse called my name and motioned me over to the scale.

After the routine weighing and measuring, I was handed the plastic urine cup with the blue lid and sent into the bathroom with verbal instructions on what to do and where to put it when finished. I was wishing their instructions included how to do this task without making a mess. After placing the cup in the secret cupboard, I washed my hands and joined the waiting nurse who then escorted me to a room to get into my paper gown and play the waiting game again.

3

PHYSICAL CONSEQUENCES

Although symptoms and possible side effects are listed on the patient form at the abortion clinics, these issues are not always discussed in detail with the patients. I am sure these conditions have to be listed for legal reasons, but you would think that doctors would also have to legally discuss these matters with the person and help them understand them more fully.

Perhaps this is an issue because only 755 clinics are available to do abortions legally. It is possible that their time is consumed with just pushing the women through the process. Maybe it is assumed that by the time women come to these clinics, the decision has been secured ..... but maybe that shouldn't be assumed. I am convinced that lives could be saved if the doctor would schedule an extra few minutes to ask some questions of the patient or make sure that the she completely understands the procedure and the possible consequences.

Many physical complications can result from the abortion procedure. Some complications are immediate such as shock, resulting from significant blood loss. When a patient goes into shock for this reason, their blood pressure lowers and their heart rate increases. Immediate treatment is critical, as once it begins, it makes itself worse.

Pelvic abscess is a very serious matter that can result in death. It is almost always caused by perforation of the uterus and many times the bowel. Hemorrhaging, which is any abnormal vaginal bleeding, can be a sign of infection. Infections can involve the uterine lining, genital tract, reproductive organs and urinary system. The onset of the infections can be characterized by nausea, vomiting, diarrhea, weakness and fever. These symptoms would bring the patient back into medical care for immediate treatment.

Other complications can happen years down the road. For instance, a post-abortive woman has a 50% higher chance of getting breast cancer, especially if performed on a woman's first pregnancy. The reasoning behind this is that the growth process of the breasts is interrupted which causes millions of cells to be at a high risk according to the Journal of the National Cancer Institute. Along with breast cancer, there is a 2.3 times higher chance of cancer of the ovaries, liver and cervix occurring. Again, this is all because of the unnatural disruption in hormones that the abortion procedure causes.

The uterus has the possibility of being punctured due to the instruments used during the procedure. Cervical lacerations or tears can occur. Abortions can result in placenta previa causing the placenta to be too close to the cervix . This can result in pre-term labor in subsequent pregnancies, many times requiring a cesarean section delivery of the baby. This condition can carry a higher risk of death and handicaps in newborns.

Pelvic inflammatory disease (inflammation of the reproductive organs) is yet another physical risk. This has many complications in itself. It can cause severe pelvic pain and cause scarring in the fallopian tubes. It is a major cause of ectopic pregnancies in which the fertilized egg remains in the fallopian tube rather than making its way to the uterus.   This can be life threatening. Pelvic inflammatory disease can also be a factor in infertility.

Another heartbreaking circumstance that can occur is miscarriage, which is the natural termination of a pregnancy. Chances of miscarrying in a future pregnancy are increased by 45% for these women. That brings on a whole new list of issues. Not only can this cause more physical complications with the risk of scar tissue building up, but there are many emotional scars caused by this event also. The woman or couple has to work through the trauma of losing a child, telling others what happened and gain courage to try again. In general, post-abortive women are in poorer health overall. Statistics show that they go to more doctor appointments than women who have not gone through this procedure.

As you can see, the risk that a woman takes is very great regarding the physical consequences. Women need to be more informed and truly understand what their future may hold in terms of illnesses and subsequent difficulties. It also needs to register within the minds of these women what they possibly may not hold in their future....a child.

4

REACTIONS

I drove home that day from my doctor appointment, numb but with flashes of emotion sparking in my mind. A quick gasp of air would rush into my lungs as fear would grab my heart. Fear of the unknown, anxiety of pain, dread of reactions and fear of truth flooded my thoughts. I pulled into the driveway, wondering how the ten mile drive had passed so quickly. I drew in a deep breath as I prepared for the rejection of my father. I knew my mom would be there. Mom was always there.

Dad was sitting at the kitchen table as I opened the glass door. I turned around to shut it and to gather one more ounce of courage. Mom walked in from the kitchen, wiping her hands on a dish towel and asked, "Did the doctor figure out what's going on?"

I nodded my head, my hands behind my back frozen to the door handle. The eyes of my parents were on me waiting for the answer.

"I'm pregnant." I held my breath now waiting for their response.

In an instant, my mom wasn't there. Without a word, she walked down the hall to the back bedroom. Tears stung my eyes as I forced my head up to look at my dad, still holding my breath and clutching the door handle. No words were spoken. He just patted his knee with his hand.

All of a sudden feeling like I was five, I sat on my daddy's knee and hugged him and told him I was sorry. My body tension released in uncontrollable crying, wishing the whole situation would go away. Dad assured me it would be okay.

Because the reactions of my parents were so opposite of what I expected, I was at a loss of what to do next. I knew I couldn't avoid my mom forever. I also knew I was the one who had to approach her. This was my doing. I couldn't play games and expect her to come to me. I walked through the hallway and peered into the guest bedroom. She was lying on the brass bed I had used when I was a little girl; her little girl, the little girl that I am sure was purposed in her mind for something different than being an unwed mother. I crawled onto the bed and rested my head on the pillow next to her. She cried. "I'm embarrassed," she whispered.

The shame was overwhelming. "I'm so sorry," my voice was barely audible. I would have rather taken a hundred beatings than to know that I had disappointed my parents. My heart ached and my neck felt swollen with the huge lump in my throat. I knew I had to face whatever came my way. I had gotten myself into this and now I had to be mature enough to shoulder the reactions and consequences.

We talked for a bit, our tones still very soft, as if the whole situation had literally taken our breath away. When finished, we left each other with a hug.

I retreated to my room as I thought about what to do next. I knew I would need to tell my boyfriend. I had just seen him the month before as I had driven to Sioux Falls, South Dakota and spent a weekend with him. I called him and explained the news. Stunned at first, he breathed a sigh and then said he would catch a bus and be in Gillette, Wyoming that weekend and we would figure things out.

When he arrived, my first response was, "I didn't know what to do. Thanks for coming to see me."

He hugged me and said, "Well, we're going to get married. That's what we're going to do." I hugged him tighter with my eyes squeezed shut, wanting to melt away. I had hoped when I opened my eyes, everything would be normal. Little did I know at that moment that very soon my life and my mind would never really feel normal again.

The next day we started making plans for a wedding. It would have to be soon, before the baby was born. My mom was a seamstress and bought patterns to make my dress and the dresses for the bridesmaids.

My dad had only one request….that I did not get married in a white dress.

5

EMOTIONAL CONSEQUENCES

Some of the physical repercussions of an abortion may be able to be repaired to the point of "feeling" okay. On the other hand some may be a daily reminder of the choice that was made.

When it comes to the emotional aspect, I believe it is harder to help post-abortive women heal. There is only so much that somebody from the outside can do. It has to be the choice of the woman to be healed. This is something that can take years to accomplish.

Many women will wear masks so well that you would never guess the inner pain they feel. The forced smile on the outside drowns out the screams that are hidden behind the eyes. Many women will not make eye contact for fear their secret will be revealed. However, others secretly beg for people to look them in the eyes. They want somebody to truly SEE them; someone who will help them to understand the pain they are feeling.

Post Abortion Syndrome, closely related to Post Traumatic Stress Disorder, will reveal itself in a number of ways. In this chapter, some of the symptoms and behaviors will be discussed to help you better understand the emotional ramifications suffered by women and, in many cases, by the men involved.

It is hard to comprehend the dark world they actually live in on a bright sunny day; the world that keeps them locked in chains. It is a world that torments them with flashbacks and a grief that seems will never go away. Depression and guilt plague them, making it a minute by minute battle on some days. Suicidal thoughts eat away at their minds as they try to understand the monster that lives inside of them that was able to allow them to do such a grisly act of violence.

Statistics show that 28% of post-abortive women later attempt suicide, many of them more than once. Because the dungeon that they reside in has chains that extend only a short distance, close relationships are hard to develop for these women because of the fear of judgment and rejection. They know, or eventually come to understand, that what they did was wrong and with the topic being so heavily debated in today's era, it is a very scary thing to admit to somebody.

Sexual dysfunction can play a big role in the lives of these women. This could be the result of a physical detriment from the abortion. As we discussed in an earlier chapter, pelvic inflammatory disease can cause a lot of discomfort during sex. The dysfunction also can be related to intimacy issues. Those issues could stem from the circumstances surrounding the terminated pregnancy. For example, if the pregnancy was a result of rape or incest, several things could trigger flashbacks of the situation.   In other instances, it could just be the fear of becoming pregnant one more time and having to be faced with a decision again.   Still another reason could also be caused by the guilt that surrounds these women which makes them feel they are not worthy of love and pleasure.

Women can also suffer insomnia and recurrent nightmares which destroy their chance for rest of any kind during the night. Sleep aids may be needed to assist them with this. Others may use background noise to try to block out the noise in their minds or to distract the nightmares that fight to enter into their rest.

Eating disorders may develop. Some women turn to food to cover up the pain. As long as they are eating, they can keep their mind off their memories. Others feel the need to punish themselves and will eat but not allow themselves to digest the food but rather force themselves to vomit (bulimia). They may also choose to not eat at all (anorexia).

These choices alone can cause many health concerns. Bulimia and anorexia can cause severe tooth decay and bring on severe problems with the heart, liver and gastrointestinal tract.   Skin conditions and dehydration can occur.   For all people, the rule stands that if we do not take care of our bodies and have a healthy balance of nutrition, every system in our physical bodies will be affected.

Panic attacks can occur at very random times. If the subject of abortion is brought up on radio or TV shows, it can cause anxiety. These times are easy to escape because the channel can just be changed. However, when the subject is brought up in a discussion or a Sunday school class or sermon, escape is not so easy.

Panic can set in because there is no way to get away from hearing truth and coming face to face with facts. A feeling of thinking that everybody knows "the secret" can be overwhelming. Seeing pictures of babies in utero can trigger a woman to think of what her baby looked like at the stage that her abortion was performed. Watching movies on the topic can bring up situations that she was previously not aware of which may add to her list of things of which she already experiences guilt.

Once a post-abortive woman comes to the point that she is willing to be healed emotionally and looks at the options available for classes to help with this, a whole new set of anxieties may present themselves. We will get into this in greater detail in a future chapter.

The woman may remember the date that her abortion was performed. She may choose to make that day or month an anniversary, forcing herself to remember each detail in a way to punish herself. Her regret will be something that makes her feel so heavy that she cannot even move. The struggle forces her to have to concentrate every moment to be able to breathe normally and hold herself together until she is in a safe place to release the tension and memories. Other times, she is not so lucky and is not able to reach that safe place on time. Then the anger, shame and hate that she has for herself is unleashed on anybody who is within her range.

Loss of self confidence is a problem that plagues these women as well. In light of their history of making poor choices, they will question themselves on decisions brought before them on many levels. Even though the decision may seem right by the five senses point of view, doubt will cause them to second guess every move they make. This may be so debilitating that they literally cannot make a decision on their own and depend on the people around them to make even the simplest of choices for them.

Because of the secrets they hold in their minds and hearts and the difficulty in forming close, healthy relationships, loneliness and isolation can overtake them. They may withdraw even from those closest to them. They don't want to be part of group gatherings. The fewer people involved in their lives, the safer their secret is.

Memories may be repressed, either as a natural defense mechanism of the body or through the aid of drugs and alcohol. In fact, abuse of this nature is four times higher in post-abortive women compared to those who choose to carry a baby to term. The use of drugs and alcohol is similar to the eating disorders in that so many other health issues can come into play. The woman at the time, however, is willing to risk it just to make the memories go away for a while.

When questioned, 98% of these women admit regret for their decision. I shared earlier that 74% of women make the choice to abort due to social reasons. They believe having the baby would be inconvenient for their life at that time. They believe their life will be better because of this decision, but statistics show 72% of the women admit that it did not improve their life. In fact, I am fully confident when I say that their lives were made worse by this choice.

One moment in time, one decision, one act that they felt was right for *them* at the time can end up causing them a life of torment that *now* affects every person with whom they come in contact. This could range from the lack of ability to form close relationships with those who cross these women's paths to the episodes that their families have to witness because of the depression and self destruction these women put themselves through.

Nervous breakdowns and psychiatric hospitalizations involve 30% of post-abortive women. The confusion these women suffer as they try to recount what would make them think that abortion was ever an option is overwhelming. This confusion causes them to second guess any future decision they make. It causes them to feel that they cannot protect the children they may have in the future because they were not able to protect the baby they aborted. They doubt themselves to the point that they can appear needy and clingy to those around them.

It concerns me when I hear women who have gone through the trauma of abortion say that it didn't bother them to do it. I know what their future holds. I know the tears they will cry. I understand the guilt that will eat away at their stomachs making them literally sick at times. I have experienced the confusion that will rip their minds to shreds, taking away any confidence they would have in making any sound choice from that point forward.

Women can turn inward and become focused on themselves and fall into the trap of self-pity. Concentration on how they have been the victim in so many areas of their lives puts the responsibility of their actions on somebody else. It is a heartbreaking day when they hit the wall that makes them stop and realize the part they played in becoming that victim.

Psalm 116:3-4
The cords of death entangled me, the anguish of the grave came over me; I was overcome by distress and sor-

row. Then I called on the name of the LORD: "LORD, save me!"

Entangled. Have you ever had the pleasure of helping to free something that has been entangled? Frustration is more like it. I recall trying to untangle a bunch of necklaces. I would randomly pull at a chain here and there. I would try to get a grip on the right piece in hopes that it might pull apart from the other strands just enough for me to wiggle a finger in to start pulling from a different angle. I would pull just to find out it was knotted onto another strand. You know that it has to be done, but it seems hopeless. It may be such a mess that you don't even know where to start.

I found two other definitions of entangled. The first one: hampered and not free. This is an accurate description of post-abortive women. They are never free from the guilt and the shame and the memories until they call out to the Lord and give it all to the One who has covered every sin in their lives. Their happiness is hampered and possibly even their joy. I personally do not believe we can ever lose our joy, but this leads into the next definition.

Entangled also means not able to act at will. Keeping focused on your joy is a choice. Being happy despite your circumstances is a choice. Many times these women are not able to act at will. Their chains are too heavy for them to move on their own. Even when they have the strength to pull at one of the chains to loosen it from the tangled mess, they run into another knot. They don't necessarily WANT to be depressed, they don't WANT to be afflicted with nightmares, but until they allow the Healing Hand to help them, their will is not their own. In these dark times, the victors of the battle are Distress and Sorrow.

Proverbs 12:25a
²⁵ Anxiety weighs down the heart,

We have all experienced this at one time or another. There are anxieties that can weigh down a heart like an anchor in the ocean. These women cannot move forward with their lives until that weight is lifted and they can truly deal with the situation at hand. More than likely, there is more to it than the act itself. There are always going to be other people involved; those that either talked them into this decision, threatened them, didn't fully inform them, didn't support them, etc. Coupled with that will be the circumstances surrounding the decision. It is never just one thing. One thing can normally be pinpointed and dealt with pretty easily. However, when you have a combination of several things, it is like the entanglement I just spoke of in Psalm 116.

The root of the problem needs to be identified. Once that is figured out, the post-abortive women have a starting point and can then deal with one thing at a time. It will be imperative that they have a support system as they deal with each emotion that surfaces. They may need a sounding board as they sort out memories, many of which may have been hidden deep inside. They will also need a strong shoulder when they deal with the facts of their abortion of which they might have been ignorant of or not wanted to admit before. These women will need people to encourage them to face and accept the truth. God's Word promises that the truth will set us free.

John 8:32
Then you will know the truth, and the truth will set you free."

Psalm 107:10-16

Some sat in darkness, in utter darkness, prisoners suffering in iron chains, because they rebelled against God's commands and despised the plans of the Most High. So he subjected them to bitter labor; they stumbled, and there was no one to help. Then they cried to the LORD in their trouble, and he saved them from their distress. He brought them out of darkness, the utter darkness, and broke away their chains. Let them give thanks to the LORD for his unfailing love and his wonderful deeds for mankind, for he breaks down gates of bronze and cuts through bars of iron.

I know it may be hard to understand how somebody can make the decision to abort their own child. If you are reading this book and have not experienced this, it is my heart to help you see these women through eyes filled with compassion. Comprehending what they are really going through in their lives can help you treat them with grace and mercy. I want you to understand that Jesus paid the same price for their sin as He did for yours.

This is truth: post-abortive women are not really living at all. They are only existing. They are prisoners suffering in chains in utter darkness. The place in which they live, in their hearts, is cold and damp. It stinks of death and rotting flesh. However, they do not have to die in that dungeon. When they choose to cry out to the Lord, He is faithful to save them from their distress. You may be that person to help free them from the dungeon and lead them to the foot of the cross where forgiveness is unleashed.

6

TANGLED WEBS

I hate when I get the cold shoulder from anyone, much less the man who would soon be my husband. He had been in Rapid City, South Dakota finding us a place to live and had come to Gillette and spent the day with my younger brother until I got off work. Being ignored was the last thing I expected from him after not seeing him for a couple of weeks.

I tried to get him to warm up but knew it was probably going to get worse as I had more news for him. Bad news. Shameful news. I joined my fiancé in the yard. "Is everything okay?" I asked.

"It was until I got here and your brother congratulated me and said that having the baby would be a great Christmas present since it is due in December," he voiced. I hung my head. I'm sure it was difficult for him to keep that inside all day. Why he was even still here at all, I didn't know. "If I have done my math correctly, I'd say that is about two months sooner than *we* should be having a baby."

He was waiting for the explanation. I had seen the doctor the day before which was the first time since my pregnancy test. The nurse had her little dial chart in hand and figured out my due date. I managed to get out to the car before the tears started. "Oh, no! Oh, no!" I had buried my face in my hands and sobbed.

Oh what tangled webs we weave in our sin! My fiancé had been in prison for a year and a half and although I wrote him and never got "involved" with anybody, I did hang out with a buddy from school with whom I had partied. Things just went a little too far one night.

"I don't know that I can raise a child that is not mine," he said, breaking the silence and sounding so final.

Panic! My mind screamed! What would I do? Nobody else is going to want me! If that is how he felt, I am sure other men would feel that way. I will be alone. I can't be alone! I just can't seem to stop disappointing people. My wedding is in a week. Invitations have been sent out and now this! What am I supposed to do? I will be humiliated yet again if I cancel the wedding.

"If you agree to get an abortion, I will marry you," he concluded.

Numbness. I lost all emotional feeling at that point. I honestly felt that I had no choice. I had no say.

I let my mom finish the details of the wedding. I didn't care. I didn't want to go to my own wedding. I couldn't get my voice to work though. I was alone. I certainly couldn't admit what was going on and the situation

I had gotten myself into. Nobody knew the turmoil stirring inside of me. I may not be good at many things, but I was a master at masking reality in my life. This was just another mask to don.

The wedding came and went. Before I knew it we had moved into our little attic apartment in Rapid City. The morning after moving in, as my new husband got ready to head for work, he handed me a telephone book and suggested that I get busy on making phone calls to find out which doctors performed abortions. I put my bathrobe on as he walked out the door. My shaking hands began fumbling through the yellow pages. My stomach hurt and I couldn't tell if it was morning sickness or nerves.

I wondered if there was any way to change his mind. I made several phone calls, but everybody said I was too far along. Maybe that would alter his thinking. I looked up a pregnancy clinic hoping that something they would show us would trigger him to understand how real this child was. When he came home I explained my findings for the day. He shrugged and walked away from me. Rejection hit me hard.

I vaguely remember going to the resource clinic and a woman visiting with both of us. My husband wouldn't budge. After a few more phone calls, I was referred to a clinic in Colorado and was informed that the cost would be $700. We made plans to go that week.

After the 350 mile trip, we entered the clinic. A clipboard was handed to me to sign waivers that I would not hold them responsible if anything went wrong. I checked the appropriate boxes. I don't remember a lot of the information on the sheet except for one detail under the heading of Possible Side Effects: death. Death?! I looked at my husband and pointed with the pen to that line. He looked and then shrugged, "It's your choice," he said with his undertone warning me that if I didn't go through with it, he would leave me.

I had two fears at that moment. The first fear was that I would die on that table. My second fear was that I would not die on that table. Even then, I knew deep down that going through with this was not going to be the end of it. I didn't know the extent of that reality, but I knew it wasn't the end. I prayed to God that He would let me die on that table so that my husband would have to explain to my to parents what happened and why I had entered such a clinic.

After handing the clipboard to the nurse, she immediately took me to a darkly lit room. It wasn't a typical patient room. It was decorated in browns, making it very dark. I looked over my shoulder pleading inside for my husband to change his mind, but he didn't move from his chair in the waiting room.

The doctor came in and explained the procedure to me. He told me he would be inserting "seaweed" into me and then would send me home (to our motel) for a few hours and then I would come back for the procedure. He handed me the gown then closed the door behind him.

I paced. I buried my face into the gown in my hands trying to stifle my tormented cries. I don't know how much time passed. I was not ready when the doctor knocked on the door. With a hint of frustration he instructed me to get ready. I obeyed and before I knew it I was dressed again and heading to the lobby. I don't remember it hurting or if I cried. I don't recall words being spoken at all. As we got back to the motel, my husband fell asleep. I paced and cried thinking about the changes that were happening to my body. I believed that my baby was dying inside of me. My husband slept. How could he sleep?

We returned to the clinic and quickly I was gowned up and moved to a very bright, sterile room. White and steel gray were the only colors I saw. I could see shiny instruments, white clothes and masks. Everything was moving very quickly.

As I was trying to take in my surroundings and fighting the panic, I felt someone straighten my right arm. The doctor scolded me as I flinched and tried to keep the IV needle from going into the vein of my hand.

That was the last thing I remember before entering into nothingness. During the groggy state of coming out of anesthesia I heard one of the doctors say, "Boy this one......" and then I was out again. Although this bothered me for many years, I finally had to hold onto the fact that maybe God plugged my ears. He knew I would have enough to deal with and would not need some tactless doctor's statement added to my situation.

The next memory I have was being in a dark room. I was thrashing around and screaming hysterically for my husband. I was disoriented and felt like I had been stuffed into a storage closet. I was sobbing uncontrollably. A nurse quickly ushered my husband into the room. As I latched onto him, still screaming, I heard the nurse warn him, "You need to get her calmed down immediately or you will both have to leave."

I wonder today about the trauma that my body must have gone through to make me behave in such a way. I have been under anesthesia since then and have never had that reaction from it. My body was responding to something.

I screamed through my gasping sobs, "Don't leave

me! Promise to never leave me!"(Our marriage lasted two and a half years).

After calming me down and getting my shakiness to subside, we left the clinic. With my right hand wrapped in gauze at the IV site, my eyes swollen from crying and still feeling very dazed, we headed back to Rapid City.

I contemplated what I would tell people. When it came time, I explained only that I lost the baby. I would leave the room or move onto another subject, leaving the person to make sense of a miscarriage occurring so far into the pregnancy.

7

HOW DO YOU SCULPT AN ELEPHANT?

In this chapter, I want to get more personal with you now that I have shared part of my story. If you are a reader who has had an abortion, by this point, you should know that I understand much of what you are going through. I know that we all handle things differently and the circumstances can vary but, spiritually, I understand the despair and hopelessness we can fall into. I know the guilt-ridden secret that lingers in our shadow which is always attached to us.

If you are a reader who is wanting to understand the lives of those who have had an abortion, I hope you are finding this information helpful. This chapter may assist you to be able to minister to them and love them through their self-condemnation.

The Scripture verses I will be using will help define what sin is and the consequences of sin. This is not to beat you up even more, but rather to show you through additional verses the hope that we have in Christ Jesus. I want you to understand that if you ask Jesus into your heart, forgiveness is yours! I encourage you to not put God into a little box. He is bigger than any sin in your life!

I know, oh, do I know, how hard it is to come face to face with sin! I have experienced first-hand, as you have seen in this book, the way condemnation can swallow you up. Please don't give up! Continue reading and grab hold of the Anchor in your storm, That Anchor is Jesus Christ. Trust that He will hold you still. Many of the verses I am sharing are known as part of the Romans Road to Salvation. These specific verses are also noted in the back of this book for an easy reference and for you to give to others as you gain the boldness to share your personal testimony.

1 John 3:4
Everyone who sins breaks the law; in fact, sin is lawlessness.

What is sin? It is deliberately and actively rejecting the boundaries that God has set for us. We have the free will to choose to sin. However, we must understand that doing so will produce consequences. The most serious of those consequences is being separated from God.

Who sins? Let's see what the Word of God tells us.

Romans 3:23
For ALL have sinned and fall short of the glory of God.

Romans 3:11
There is no one righteous, not even one; there is no one who understands; there is no one who seeks God.

Do you see it? ALL have sinned. It is not just you. So often we think that we are the only one in the world who has committed a sin and that we are not worthy of God's forgiveness.

The thoughts that wandered through my mind were, "Well, I know God could forgive others, but my sin is bigger than theirs." How arrogant to think that my sin was bigger than my God! There is NO ONE righteous.

We fall so easily into that trap of comparing ourselves to others. Satan knows our weaknesses and he will take every opportunity he can to point out our flaws and then show us somebody who "appears" better in that area so that we can feel inferior. I started realizing that everybody had a story. Everybody has sin in their lives and their own set of insecurities for which they are trying to compensate.

Like I said at the beginning of this book, when I started telling my story, many women came up to me and said they had been through the same thing. These women were people I knew and to whom I had been comparing myself.

There are so many hurting people in this world who are all around you. No matter what you have been through, you have an opportunity to be healed. Through that restoration process, you can become strong so that you can help heal other broken hearts within your sphere of influence.

Genesis 4:6-7.
⁶ Then the LORD said to Cain, "Why are you angry? Why is your face downcast? ⁷ If you do what is right, will

you not be accepted? But if you do not do what is right, sin is crouching at your door; it desires to have you, but you must rule over it. "

One of the things, as post-abortive women, that we may be angry about is what we would consider as deception. We may not have felt we were given enough information. Focusing on the broken promises can infuriate us. We might try to blame the rejection and lack of support from others. Our own ignorance and weakness in the situation may disgust us. Anger about the pressure that we received from others can overwhelm us. We may even be directing this emotion towards God, perhaps feeling punished by Him. Anxiety that God might take one of our other children or that He may not allow us to conceive a child again can torment our minds.

A local pastor shared his experience of being called in as a hospital chaplain to visit a young couple that were close to having a baby. The woman was very distraught. Not understanding fully her response to what should be a joyous occasion, the chaplain took a chance and asked if she had a history of abortion. She hung her head, nodded and confessed, "I'm afraid that God is going to punish me by taking this child or causing it to have deformities."

The reasons that we have to be angry may be good reasons, but that emotion can begin to rule over us. The emotion of anger does not necessarily have to be exhibited by fits of rage. It can come out in a variety of ways and it can fester and eat away at other areas of our lives.

The silent treatment can be used against the people who are directly involved. We may withhold affection from these people, as a way to punish them. This can become such a habit that it can cause us to be very withdrawn from everybody. Our quiet world can become our only safe place.

Becoming critical of others can be a way of feeling superior. If we can find enough faults in other people, it will make us feel that we really aren't that bad of a person for what we've done. Our çritical and judgmental behavior will push people away from us, putting us back into our comfort zone of our shielded, reserved world.

We may choose to act out in disrespectful ways. Submissiveness may be the last quality we feel we owe anybody because of what we have gone through. A heart of unforgiveness is nurtured by all of this behavior. Anger can convince us that everybody is against us. As that negative root buries itself deep into our hearts, we begin to believe that we are the only victim in the situation.

These reactions can be very destructive. They can cause hurt to others, whether they were directly involved in the situation or not. If we do not learn to deal with our anger correctly, it can lead to greater and increased sin. Let me show you what God's Word mentions about anger.

Proverbs 29:11
Fools give full vent to their rage, but the wise bring calm in the end.

Ecclesiastes 7:9
Do not be quickly provoked in your spirit, for anger resides in the lap of fools.

James 1:19-20
My dear brothers and sisters, take note of this: Everyone should be quick to listen, slow to speak and

slow to become angry, because human anger does not produce the righteousness that God desires.

Ephesians 4:26-27
"In your anger do not sin": Do not let the sun go down while you are still angry, and do not give the devil a foothold.

Ephesians 4:31
Get rid of all bitterness, rage and anger, brawling and slander, along with every form of malice.

Psalm 37:8
Refrain from anger and turn from wrath; do not fret—it leads only to evil.

Anger gives the devil a foothold and out of greed, he will take more and more from our hearts, minds and lives. If we do not pay close attention, anger can become a way of life. It is hard to break habits of being bitter and resentful. It is a choice to put away anger and bitterness.

Proverbs 6:16-19
There are six things the Lord hates, seven that are detestable to him: haughty eyes, a lying tongue, hands that shed innocent blood, a heart that devises wicked schemes, feet that are quick to rush into evil, a false witness who pours out lies and a person who stirs up conflict in the community.

Exodus 20:13
"You shall not murder.

God is a God of love. Although there may be natural consequences (the physical and emotional detriments of the abortion), God still loves us. It is the sin at which He directs His anger. Sin causes a righteous (morally justifiable) anger in God. Do you remember what we read in Genesis 4? God says we must rule over sin or master it. It is something that can be achieved.

Romans 12:19
Do not take revenge, my dear friends, but leave room for God's wrath, for it is written: "It is mine to avenge; I will repay," says the Lord.

Vengeance belongs to God. What freedom this verse brought to me! We need to understand that we don't have to be in charge of planning how to get revenge on somebody else who may have been involved in our situation. That can be left in God's hands. He is a just God and knowing that can assist us in forgiving others that were involved. Coming to terms with what we have done and comprehending that God is willing to forgive us for that may help us to be more compassionate with other people. It makes us see how petty we can be in the things we allow to anger us.

Let's continue and see what sin can do with respect to our relationship with God.

Isaiah 59:2
But your iniquities have separated you from your God; your sins have hidden his face from you, so that he will not hear.

When I first read that God would not hear me, it scared me. I rely on my God for everything and to think that He would not hear me when I called out to Him made me change my ways of prayer. It became important to begin my prayer time by asking God to cleanse my heart. If there is sin in my heart or in my thought life, I ask Him to remove it and to forgive me. I want to keep my relationship constantly restored.

Many times we try to justify our sin so that we can get away from the guilt. Rationalizing our sin becomes a coping mechanism. In our situation of abortion, we can buy into the belief that it wasn't a baby we killed, but rather it was just a cluster of cells we were eliminating from our bodies. We can rationalize that this was our only option. It was "best for everyone involved." It then becomes okay and if it is okay then we don't have to feel guilty for having done it.

But it's not okay. It's not okay to sin and it's not okay to justify it. As long as we continue to justify it, we will never be at a point that we can face the reality of what we did and begin to deal with it and heal from it. However, there is hope.

Romans 6:23
For the wages of sin is death, but the free gift of God is eternal life through Christ Jesus our Lord.

The sin that we committed deserves death. God has given us a gift though; His Son, Jesus Christ. He died for our sins so that we don't have to. These next verses are going to tell you how easy it is to claim that gift of eternal life and the benefits of it.

Romans 5:8

But God showed his great love for us by sending Christ to die for us while we were still sinners

Romans 10:9-10 and 13

If you confess with your mouth that Jesus is Lord and believe in your heart that God raised him from the dead, you will be saved. For it is by believing in your heart that you are made right with God, and it is by confessing with your mouth that you are saved, For "Everyone who calls on the name of the Lord will be saved.

It truly is that simple! Confess with your mouth and believe in your heart. Many of you may have already taken this step. So often we forget the benefits of being a child of God. We get so focused on the sin in our lives and issues from our past that we forget that God said we are fearfully and wonderfully made. Look at the following verses and remind yourself what you possess because you are in the family of God.

Romans 8:6

The mind governed by the flesh is death, but the mind governed by the Spirit is life and peace.

Romans 5:1

Therefore, since we have been made right in God's sight by faith, we have peace with God because of what Jesus Christ our Lord has done for us.

Peace is ours! What did Jesus Christ do for us? He died for our sins. Because of that, we have peace!

Romans 8:1
So now there is no condemnation for those who belong to Christ Jesus.

We do not have to live a life constantly condemning
ourselves for the wrong things we have done and the bad
choices we have made. When we live in condemnation, we
reject the gift of God and chain ourselves up and live in
bondage. The truth is that we are children of God. He is
our Father.

Psalm 32:5
**Then I acknowledged my sin to you and did not
cover up my iniquity. I said, "I will confess my transgressions to the Lord." And You forgave the GUILT of
my sin.**

Jesus is the only One who can forgive sins and wipe
our slates clean, but we have to be open with Him and not
try to cover our sins. We have to trust God enough and
come to Him boldly and then rejoice in the fact that He not
only forgives our sins but forgives us from the GUILT of
our sin. That was a powerful statement to me when I discovered it. I had no doubt that God had forgiven me but I
could not shed that guilt. He can take that away too. That's
how big our God is!

When we ask Christ into our hearts and when we
have confessed and repented from our sin, we want to
start living in a more righteous manner. Sin needs to be
whittled away, but we have to be able to identify sin. You
may have heard the story of the sculptor. When he is asked
what he is sculpting, he replies, "An elephant."

The other man then asks, "How do you sculpt an elephant?"

The sculptor considers the question and then says: "It's really very simple. You just chip away anything that doesn't look like an elephant."

As we surrender to God's Holy work in us He starts chipping away the sin in our lives. He chips away anything that does not look like Him and that does not express His holy character. It is a lifelong process, even according to the most well-known evangelists. However, once we take the steps to move forward in our spiritual walk, we have an assurance beyond measure. Take a look at this beautiful and hope-filled promise from God's Word:

Romans 8:38-39
And I am convinced that nothing can ever separate us from God's love. Neither death nor life, neither angels nor demons, neither our fears for today nor our worries about tomorrow—not even the powers of hell can separate us from God's love. No power in the sky above or in the earth below—indeed, nothing in all creation will ever be able to separate us from the love of God that is revealed in Christ Jesus our Lord.

THAT is a Father's love! Can you see how deep that love is and how powerful it is? He knows what we have done. He understands who we are. The beautiful news is that He loves us anyway. Genesis 16:13 says He is the God who sees me. Isn't that great? I don't have to pretend. My masks don't have to be worn around God because He sees me, the real me, and He loves me.

We live in a world wherein love can be very conditional so we get accustomed to having to earn love. God's love is unconditional. There is nothing we can do to earn it. Don't waste any more time. There is a gift waiting for you. Reach out and accept it!

SECRETS KEPT

Brown, like muddy water churning under

Trampling feet

Causing minds to race in circles

"What's the truth today?"

The heart struggling to keep beating,

Pumping blood hard as every vessel desires to shut down.

Wondering, always wondering.

Nowhere safe to cry

Nowhere safe to turn

Put on a smile, SECRETS KEPT

Keep moving, SECRETS KEPT

Breathe . . . . . Breathe . . . . . Breathe . . . . .

SECRETS...

KEPT

By JoEllen Claypool

8

HIDE AND SEEK

For the next year and a half I hid. I buried myself in my work. At one point, I was working four different jobs at the same time. In the mornings I worked as a secretary at an office. I would then go directly to my job as a transcriptionist in a psychiatrist's office. Right after that my shift at the pizza parlor commenced. Then on the side, I managed to find time to be a salesperson.

I felt I was leading a double life as Wednesday nights and Sundays were reserved for Bible study, but the rest of the week I hid behind alcohol and drugs. During any free time or days off, my husband and I would party. Our suppers would consist of the different happy hours offered at the bars each night of the week. As long as we were partying, we got along. My husband worked at a motel restaurant/bar. He knew a lot of the musical groups that would come through so after I was done with my evening job I would meet up with him at his job and we would party with the bands.

I hid. I didn't care if I was ever found. If I started to feel any sort of emotion, I hid. If I started to remember, I hid. Everything became a blur. The next clear memory I had was January of 1990 when my husband talked me into going to the doctor. He was convinced that my moodiness was different than normal and predicted that I was pregnant. He was right. I was two months along.

That baby saved my life. I know he did. As soon as I heard the news, there were no more drugs and no more drinking. He turned my thinking around to more positive intentions. I felt I was being given a second chance that I didn't deserve. I started taking care of myself. I spent as much time as I could with my Bible study buddies. My husband and I started spending less time together as I could no longer participate in the activities in which he was involved.

I recall one Wednesday night in particular. I was waiting for my ride to Bible study when there was a knock on our door. Opening the door, I stood in front of a police officer. He asked for my husband. I explained that he was at a basketball game. He pushed a button on his shoulder and radioed the information in to the station. What I heard next made my blood run cold.

"If it is the wife you are speaking to, bring her in. There is a warrant out for her arrest," the voice on the other end instructed.

The officer put his right hand on my left elbow as he gently led me from our apartment. The officer was very compassionate. I don't know if it was because of the tears or the picture of "innocence" before him of a young lady who looked like she should be on the cover of a magazine for mommies. I was dressed in a cute little blue and white maternity dress with an obvious baby bump and my long hair was pulled up in a blue bow. At any rate, he explained that he would not put me in handcuffs. Just as he was helping me into the back seat, my ride showed up. I explained to the older couple what was happening. They said they would relay the message to our pastor.

After finding out that I was being booked on charges for bad checks, my mind was reeling. I was always very careful with my bank accounts. (I found out later that my husband had taken checks from the back of my checkbook and forged my signature causing numerous checks to come through my account and bounce due to the insufficient funds).

In the middle of fingerprinting, my pastor walked in so that he could post bail for me. I could chalk that up under one of my most humiliating lifetime experiences ever.

He drove me back to his house where we were having our weekly meeting. He was trying to encourage me the best he could on the way. I was able to get out of the car when we arrived. I stood next to the car, but my feet felt frozen to the ground.

I could see everybody waiting in the living room. A couple of the women came out and loved on me, reminding me that they were all there for me. People were trying to break into my life. It was so hard to trust people. I would let them break down my walls just a little bit at a time.

When I had my son in July, I could not get over how perfect he was. Ten little fingers and ten little toes were all in the right place. He was flawless. Everything about that baby made me want to be a better person. I poured my heart into him.

I was very thankful I had my child because I did not have my husband. He became very involved in gambling and still wanted to party. Being a dad didn't fit into his schedule. I ended up moving back home with my parents in Wyoming and going through a divorce in 1991.

After having been there for a while, my folks and I were visiting during a family dinner. I am not sure what was said that I found so humorous, but I started to laugh. It was a genuine, spur of the moment laugh. My dad stopped and looked at me. My attention turned to him. His chin was quivering and he said, "There you are."

My laughter slowed down and I asked, "What do you mean?"

My dad continued, "You've been gone for so long." His comment startled me.

A few things hit me at that moment. I didn't know that I had been any different. I had no idea that I had withdrawn into myself that much. I also had not realized I had drawn other people into my world. The people who cared about me and loved me had been worried about me.

My dad was able to notice in an instant when I began to break out of my chains. For a dad, what a glorious day of relief that must have been!

As a mother of adult children now, I know the joy that was leaping in his heart at that moment. I have watched my children closely as they struggled with adulthood and, at times, depression. I worried about whether they were going to give up or not. It's a terrible feeling, knowing that all you can do is sit back and watch, being ready when they need you. Then the day comes when there is a smile on their face and they laugh and I find myself just wanting to be silly and say funny things just to see them laugh again and again.

Seeing me laugh again must have filled my parents with hope; a hope that assured them that everything would be okay. For me, it was only the beginning of learning to live again.

9

THE HEART OF A MAN

About fifteen years ago I started becoming very aware of the fact that God brings people across our path for a reason. I am very watchful when I meet someone new. I may have something to offer them or they may have something to teach me. I was about half way through writing this book when a new friend of mine briefly shared her experience involving a past abortion and how she was now involved in a ministry with other women surrounding that issue.

I met this woman and her husband when they came to the church that my new husband pastored. They were staying at the campground up the road. When the couple came in, the first thing she said to me was, "We are here for four weeks, where can we be used?"

I loved her instantly. She had such a sweet and gentle countenance. She was a worker. She loved the Lord and shared her musical talents with us and we have kept in contact ever since. I knew from the moment we shook hands, there was a connection.

I did not know it at that time, but this woman had been sharing her testimony of her abortion experience. She was sharing with others regarding God's forgiveness for her sin and deliverance from her guilt and shame. She had been doing this for years prior to the writing of this book.

The day her story was revealed to me, I knew why she was brought across my path. She would be helping me with this book by editing and writing my foreword and sharing more of her story.

However, the Lord didn't stop there. He had also brought another family into our lives through our civil war re-enacting unit. My initial thought as to why our paths crossed was revealed the first day we met. We had gone to chapel time at our event and the chaplain stated that this would be his last time preaching for the re-enactments. Right away, the captain of our unit wanted my husband, Dallas, to move into the position. Dallas considered this time as his break from preaching so did not jump at the opportunity.

That afternoon, the new family was visiting with us. We had a lot in common and it was easy to talk to them. The husband described that he felt his gift was evangelism. Dallas and I looked at each other. Bingo! God is good! Dallas encouraged him to be the new chaplain and that was the end of the matter.

Two years into our relationship with this family, they were passing through our area and stopped to visit which "just happened to be" in the middle of this book project.

We were around the dining table discussing things from our past. The husband had been talking about revealing his secrets to his fiancé. Through the background noise and the visiting, I thought I heard the word abortion. There were lots of little ears around though and it was not mentioned again.

I wondered for days if I had heard correctly. I just knew, with the timing of it all, that God had orchestrated this. The more I thought about it, the more I knew that a section about men needed to be included in this book. So often we hear about the act of abortion itself and we hear some of the women's stories but very seldom do we remember the men involved. This is their child too and it is their loss as well.

Making the decision to be brave, I emailed his wife about the topic. She wrote back promptly and verified what I had heard. I asked her if she would mind me sending him some interview questions. I opened up for the first time with her about my book idea and asked if she thought he might be willing to include his input.

At our next re-enactment, Danny apologized for not having filled out the form but said that he would be willing to sit down and talk to me during the event in our free time. We made the time to do that. Through tears and sobs he told me his story.

As a young man, still in school, Danny found himself as an expectant father with his young girlfriend. Although wanting to do the right thing to provide for the woman and child, pressure came from the parents of the girl to abort the baby. Not feeling that he had any say in the matter, an abortion was performed. Danny said the relationship was never really the same after that and it did not work out for them.

Moving on with his life and through other relationships, Danny got involved with another young woman. During the course of this relationship, a woman from his recent past called him and said that she was pregnant with his child. She stated that she needed money for an abortion that was scheduled for early the next morning.

Danny delivered the money to her but throughout that night, he was not able to rest. Very early the following morning, Danny rushed to the woman's house to get the money back. He knew he could not in good conscience pay for this procedure. When he got there, she said the abortion had already been completed "I didn't believe her. She didn't look like she had gone through anything. It was so early, she couldn't have had it done that morning. Nothing felt right. I felt she was lying to me and that she was only after the money," Danny remembered.

Then he paused, and the tears flowed. "But it didn't matter. I had given her the money even though I knew what it was going to be used for. As far as I was concerned, it was blood money." He paused. He grimaced and hung his head as he finished. "I was willing to kill my own child….and it sickens me."

As his relationship deepened with his new girlfriend and plans for marriage were made, these choices began to haunt him. He could not enter into this marriage with the baggage and secrets he had hidden in his heart. He had to be honest with her.

He was fully prepared for her to cancel the wedding. He confessed to her that he was not what she thought he was. He told her he was capable of unspeakable things. He admitted his role in the acts of these abortions, preparing for the worst. The reaction was not what was expected. Instead of judging, turning and running the other way, Danny's fiancé was able to see his hurt and how deeply it had affected him. She knew he was repentant of these decisions. She offered him love, acceptance and compassion, although Danny, just like post-abortive women, didn't feel worthy of such acts of goodness.

The men that have abortion attached to their past can suffer much of the same symptoms that the women do. Because of the view of men as protectors, this is a major issue that attacks the minds of these fathers. Whether they were in agreement or not to follow through with the abortion, they can feel "less than" because they were not able to stand up and protect their child and provide for the baby.

One post-abortive man felt overwhelming emotions over this concept. He knew that his child had been entrusted in his care and he had failed to protect his baby. He stated, "It created a domino effect of bad choices."

Our society can also place the pressure on a man to suppress his grief. In order to cope with the loss of their child, some of the symptoms men may exhibit are silence (keeping their grief "secret") and/or involvement with addictions.

Confusion can block the truth in the minds of men as well. One man was said to be "handling" the abortion he encouraged his ex-wife, Debi, to have "in his own way." Debi confirms, "There is only *one* way to deal with the sin of abortion. It is the same way you deal with any sin; by turning to Jesus Christ. To think it can be dealt with any other way is self-deception." This man has not made that step yet and is furious that his ex-wife is being transparent about the abortion while she tries to help others with the issue even though she has left his name out of it.

My husband, Dallas, and I married in 1996. He is the father of the baby that I aborted. He had no idea that I had even been pregnant. Shortly after my divorce from my former husband, I saw Dallas at the grocery store in my hometown He approached me and asked where I had been for the last few years.

"You just disappeared! I tried getting a hold of you and your friend told me you had gotten married?!" His excitement to see me sent my mind reeling.

I paid for my groceries and held out my shaky hand to receive my change then we walked outside together.

"Why did you leave?" Dallas asked.

I felt like I was going to be sick. Every muscle in my body seemed to tremble as I searched for the right words to say. "I was pregnant," I carefully whispered.

"Would you like to go get a cup of coffee?" The gentleness in his voice soothed my nerves.

We met at a restaurant across town. He asked why I looked shaken when I had seen him.

"It caught me off guard," I explained. "I never dreamed I would see you again and have to tell you what happened." I confessed what the events and he knew right away what I was getting at.

"Was it mine?" Dallas asked.

"Yes." He directed no anger towards me. He passed no judgment. He only expressed how glad he was to have found me again.

The Lord reveals to me new information about my abortion each year. He knows I couldn't handle all of the facts at once. It hit me as I was writing this chapter that Dallas was a father who was not given a choice. I did not provide him an opportunity to have any say in the matter. I hadn't informed him of my condition. I know that I have apologized to him for my actions, but it never crossed my mind before that he was not even given a chance to weigh in on the decision regarding his own child. It broke my heart for him and made me realize how self-absorbed I had been.

Dallas reflected back on his own views of abortion when I asked. He couldn't really remember thinking much about it one way or the other before he was 30. He did encourage the mother of his third child to abort the baby that was growing inside of her. He felt he had no business being with her in the first place.

When asked about his views about that particular incident today, he responded, "I praise God every day that she was raised by parents who surrounded her with love and support and that she listened to them. She now has raised a beautiful boy who is 18 years old. Today I truly see and understand what that girl's family saved her from. Not only did she get to experience the joy of having a son, but they saved her from a life of uncertainty, of guilt and shame over having killed another human who was helpless and defenseless."

As my husband wrote out the rest of his response, he shared, "I know that the woman I have been married to for the past 17 years felt pressured and gave in to that pressure by her first husband to abort a child. She has never been the same since. I have stood by and watched her torture herself, question herself and hate herself because of one decision. The wounds and scars are so deep that I, at first, had no idea how to help her. I wanted and felt the need to fix it but found I couldn't."

For men who are fixers, not being able to fix a situation is incredibly frustrating. My husband admitted that he doesn't pretend to understand what I or millions of other women go through each day and each year as the anniversary date of the death of our unborn child comes. What he does understand, however, and has no problem sharing with me or others, is that "through God's grace and mercy, forgiveness and peace can be obtained as we talk about it, pray about it, and, for sure, share with others."

"They are not alone and they don't have to be held hostage by their past," Dallas assures.

Dallas finished up his interview questionnaire with such encouraging words to me that it melted my heart. I am so ashamed of the things I have put him through as I struggled to deal with this issue in my life. How he was ever able to endure, I will never be able to comprehend.

He ends with, "I am so proud of JoEllen as she has done the hard work to understand that she has been forgiven and that one day she will be reunited with our child in heaven. Each day is better than the one before as she works through sharing with others either to prevent someone from making this mistake or showing them there is a possibility of having a rich, full, forgiven life after making this decision. Good job sweetheart and keep on keeping on."

That's all we can do some days is just keep on keeping on.

10

A TIME TO HEAL

Ecclesiastes 3:1-8

1 There is a time for everything, and a season for every activity under heaven: 2 a time to be born and a time to die, a time to plant and a time to uproot, 3 a time to kill and a time to heal, a time to tear down and a time to build, 4 a time to weep and a time to laugh, a time to mourn and a time to dance, 5 a time to scatter stones and a time to gather them, a time to embrace and a time to refrain, 6 a time to search and a time to give up, a time to keep and a time to throw away, 7 a time to tear and a time to mend, a time to be silent and a time to speak, 8 a time to love and a time to hate, a time for war and a time for peace.

My friend, Sheila, reminded me and so beautifully stated that "There is an ordained time to heal. It's part of God's plan and His goodness to all of us." That ordained time becomes such a precious moment in one's life after the chaos.

The point had come for me to start breaking out of my chaos. Now that I was starting to live again, it meant I was starting to feel again. Shortly after Dallas and I got married we became pregnant, but it resulted in a miscarriage. I couldn't help but think of the Bible event of King David and Bathsheba losing their first baby after David had sinned against the Lord.

Living became very painful. September (the month in which I had the abortion) became the month I did not want to live anymore. It became a month that was cursed for me. It *seemed* that everything bad that happened would take place during the month of September. No, I was not very fond of that month at all.

Beginning in late July of every year I would start to brace myself, the tension in my body causing constant headaches. At the end of August, I would draw in one more deep breath and would not let it out until I made it safely through September.

September 1 would arrive. I would make myself relive every moment, every fear, smell, and pain of the day that I had my abortion as a way to punish myself. I would be agitated with everyone around me.

The following two pages contain a poem that I wrote in the midst of my chaos. Poetry has always been a vent for me and it helps me to unclutter my mind. The different fonts are intentional for added expression.

October

Like a breath of fresh air

I absorb the relief that October brings me.

I stretch my arms wide welcoming life again, hugging it closely.

A new year begins and every fiber in me relaxes

like a puppet with no master,

Finally convinced my mind can focus once more.

I can now appreciate color and sounds again

as I emerge from the dark cold dungeon

of September .

Cursed are you, September, for no good thing comes from you.

You add nothing to my message.

You rob me of my peace,

as each year your bony fingers try to wrap around my heart and squeeze the life from it.

You poison my mind with the cruelest of intentions,
having no regard for others at all.

Cursed are you, September, for the evil you stir up in
your autumn winds,

A different heartache clinging to each leaf that falls
in my midst.

But the winds of change are coming.

My sweet October's near.

And it brings me victory over you once again.

And I will rise up on wings of eagles and soar high above you
and see how small and powerless you really are.

Poor September, your efforts of control are so short lived.

Ahhhh!

Like a breath of fresh air,

I absorb you October!

By JoEllen Claypool

October could never come soon enough. Every year I wondered if September would win the final war. When I would crawl into bed at night, tears would drench my pillow. Sleep, if it came at all during that month, was very disrupted, full of nightmares and sleep walking. I would revert back to behavior I experienced shortly after the abortion, namely searching through the bed covers thinking my baby was lost in the sea of blankets. I would panic when I couldn't find her. I struggle to this day, periodically waking at night searching the house for somebody that "should be there."

Thoughts of suicide during this time would flood my waking hours. Darkness would overcome me and I wanted to walk into it until I disappeared.

When I would be alone, the silence was not kind to me. In fact, it was deafening with all of the insults and accusations that hurled themselves inside of me. I slept with the TV on at night to try to drown out the inner chaos. I just wanted it to stop.

During one dark moment, I went into the bathroom one morning. I saw a razor blade laying on the medicine cabinet. I took it between my fingers and rubbed my thumb against the cool smoothness of it. I put it in my pocket and walked into the back yard. I wandered around a bit and noticed that no matter where I was, Dallas was not too far from me. He busied himself with yard work and peered up every once in a while. I knew he was keeping an eye on me.

I moved to the fence marking the boundary lines of our property. I closed my eyes and thought of the things I would miss. My husband, kids and family, of course, were the first things that came to my mind. I felt the hot sun on my face. I would miss that. I shivered as the gentle breeze fingered its way through my hair. I heard the familiar buzz of the cars on the interstate. I would even miss those things, but could they ever be bigger than my pain? In the middle of my torment, I couldn't see how.

I removed the razor blade from my pocket. A strange thought crossed my mind. I have two wrists, I would need two blades. That idea had no sooner left my thinking when I had loosened my grip only a bit on the blade, enough for it to slide sideways and reveal two blades.

I started to shake as I felt the devil, himself, wrapping his arms around me and "supplying my needs" and whispering encouragement in my ears to follow through with his plan. I was on the verge of panic as I turned and walked towards my husband. My numb legs managed to find their way to him and I held onto him as I wept. I felt so weak, physically and mentally. I went into the house and threw the two blades in the garbage.

I believe God gave me a dream that night to take the thoughts of suicide away from me. In my dream, I was sitting on my couch. I had taken a handful of pills and swallowed them. Right after I had done that, my two youngest boys, then 5 and 8 years old, came and sat by me on the couch. I realized, in anguish, that I could not reverse the decision I had just made. I cried with them, telling them how sorry I was as I slowly faded into the nothingness that I thought I desired. It has been several years since that dream occurred but I can remember it as if I had it this morning.

As the months before July would approach, I would try to change my thoughts if I started thinking about the abortion. For a long time, if I heard news casts about abortions, I would turn off the TV. In 2004, however, I started forcing myself to listen. I would cry and cry.

I hated myself. It made me sick to think that I was capable of doing something so hideous. I couldn't look myself in the eye, much less other people. I felt if others knew, they would judge me. I didn't know who that person was that had the abortion because it went against anything I ever believed in.

I despised going to the doctors' offices now and filling out their redundant paperwork for my yearly exam because they always asked the number of pregnancies and the number of births. I wanted to lie but didn't know if they would be able to tell. I would hang my head when the doctor would ask me and I would mumble the answer.

In church discussions I didn't feel that I could offer anything when the discussion of abortion surfaced. Of course I was against it, but how could I say that knowing that I went through with one? How hypocritical.

I was listening to the radio one afternoon as I was sitting in our kitchen. A woman was describing her experience of a past abortion. On a commercial break, an announcement came on advertising Healing Hearts, a class for post-abortive women held at a local Pregnancy Resource Center. I didn't have a clue that there were groups that could help someone like me. I shakily took my phone and dialed the number that was announced.

A sweet, gentle tone came through the receiver. I pushed my voice out enough to let her know why I was calling. Her sympathetic tone drew me in and I let her explain the Healing Hearts program to me. She let me know that it was an intense, 11 week Bible study that would help me come to terms with what I had done. She assured me that I would be able to find the forgiveness that I was searching for.

I let Dallas know that this was something I wanted to

do. He was very supportive, but I had to give him some instructions. I told him that I did not want him coddling me through this time of healing. This was something I had to face on my own. I didn't want him feeling sorry for me because I was not the victim in this situation; our baby was.

I was not prepared for the level of intensity that this study had in store. It lacked mercy on revealing facts to me but also showed me where mercy could be found: at the foot of the cross of Jesus Christ. It lacked compassion with its vivid details but reminded me Who had compassion on my soul. This study was unforgiving when it came to excuses but revealed the Father of forgiveness in a whole new light.

There was nothing easy about this course and my husband stayed true to his promise and did not coddle me. Every time I learned a new detail, I would grab my stomach feeling like I would be sick. Many times I wanted to give up on the class. There were times I didn't think I could take any more.

There were so many verses that impacted my life during this time; verses I could personally relate to and others that filled me with the hope that I needed in order to continue living.

Psalm 38:4
My guilt has overwhelmed me like a burden too heavy to bear.

Psalm 34:4-5
I sought the LORD, and he answered me; he delivered me from all my fears. Those who look to him are radiant; their faces are never covered with shame.

The verse that became my life verse was found in Leviticus.

Leviticus 26:13b
I broke the bars of your yoke and enabled you to walk with your heads held high.

Out of my shame, I hid like Adam and Eve had done in the Garden of Eden. I didn't want God to find me because I couldn't hold my head up. How was I supposed to look Him in the eye after I destroyed something that He knit together inside of me? (Psalm 139:13)

About half way through the study, I had another very vivid nightmare. It seemed that I was awake. It was dark with only the faint illumination of the hall light allowing me to see anything at all. There was a dark shadow standing next to my bed. Before I understood what was happening, it reached down and grabbed me by the hair at the back of my head. In an instant, I was in front of our closet doors which were both full length mirrors. The figure slammed my cheek against the mirror. In a harsh whisper, I heard, "You don't have the courage to face what you've done. You can't even look yourself in the eye, much less anybody else." I woke up suddenly, my heart beating so hard I thought it would awaken my husband. I was afraid to go back to sleep. I remained in bed but stayed alert until it was time to get up.

I went into the bathroom to begin getting ready for the day. I was brushing my hair and realized that I was focusing on my hair, not looking at my face. The words in the nightmare came back to me. I didn't want to believe it so decided to test it. I moved closer to the mirror. I slowly moved my eyes from looking at my hair, to my chin, to my nose then finally into the blue of my eyes. I immediately broke into tears but did not break my gaze. I knew the secrets that those eyes held. It seemed if you could find the combination to the safe behind those eyes, you could enter a dimension that nobody had ever visited.

This incident made me more determined than ever to face my past. I couldn't grow anymore or be used to my fullest extent until I dealt with this issue.

James 5:16
Therefore confess your sins to each other and pray for each other so that you may be healed. The prayer of a righteous person is powerful and effective.

I knew I needed to pray for strength. Our small Healing Hearts group had become a very safe place for me. The King's scepter of peace was being extended to me, giving me permission to approach. I only needed to reach out and grasp the promise of that peace.

Through the class, I discovered so much about myself. My ex-husband called one day during this time. He scolded me for being short tempered with him on the phone. Very calmly, I responded, "You should feel lucky that I am using a civil tongue with you at all. I am dealing with some things from our past right now and it is probably not a good day to talk with me."

He immediately knew what I was talking about and his tone softened with me. It was clear that it weighed on his mind also after all these years. He told me he was sorry and my heart fell. Thoughts raced through my mind, "Not now. Don't tell me that now!"

He said that it was the most selfish act he had committed. He also said that he had acted without conscience and with disregard for me and that he had no right to put me through it. He said if he had it to do over again, he would do it differently and for just a split second, I had a hope fill my heart. For an instant, I was back at that time. I was going to have my baby and then, just as quickly, realized it was too late. Hopeless tears flowed.

I took advantage of this opportunity to fill in some of the blanks on my study sheet for that week. I asked my ex-husband what my behavior was like after the abortion. I literally had no memories of our time together for months afterwards.

He quietly said, "You weren't there. You would give only one word answers. You were gone." He continued to explain, "You were very distant, like you were drugged or in another place. You put your emotions aside and chose not to deal with it. You were always looking for assurance from me. You wanted to be left alone but you didn't want to be alone."

I couldn't help but cry as I mourned the loss of my time. I had no recollection of anything that he was telling me. However, remembering my dad's words that I "was back", confirmed that what he was saying was true.

I felt such regret for not being strong enough to stand up for myself and defend my child. I still worry about that with my kids today. I feel I won't be able to protect them. I don't like knowing that my kids will feel any sense of fear or pain. To know that I caused pain and fear in my baby makes me sick.

Oh, if I had only been stronger, things could have been so different. That regret can be almost too much to bear at times as I realize I will never have my child with me on this earth. I do believe, however, that I will be reunited with my child in heaven.

Psalm 27:10
Though my father and mother forsake me, the LORD will receive me.

I had to deal with the anger that filled my heart. Anger towards my former husband burned within me for promising that he would stay with me and then didn't. I was disgusted with myself because of my weakness and allowing someone else to control me. Through my irritation, I wanted to cast blame on the clinic for minimizing the situation and for not explaining in detail what I was actually doing.

I had to figure out how to allow myself to feel loved and accepted by God after what I had done. I didn't feel worthy of His presence and deliverance but God reminded me not to limit Him and not to put Him in a box. I was so humbled that He would even consider forgiving me.

I finished the Healing Hearts class and even shared my testimony at a fundraising dinner for the Pregnancy Resource Center. Even though I knew I was healed and forgiven, it didn't mean I forgot. The memories and pain never go away. Although my depression wasn't as severe, my body seemed to be in such a routine of going through that every year, I would still get tense starting in July. Doing some of the research for this book project helped me to understand that what I was experiencing was the post-abortive syndrome that we discussed earlier. My husband was very patient with me and would assure me in mid-September that the month was almost over.

Dallas had introduced a Bible study to our church. It was very in depth. The third book of the study was learning how to tell our testimonies to people. At this point he decided to implement a study he had written regarding forgiveness. He explained that it would entail coming face to face with some things that we may have repressed for a long time and having to write a letter to our offender (not that we had to send it but just to get the words out as if we were going to send it). He allowed people to opt out of this section of the class but approached me and encouraged me to deal with this issue once and for all. Sometimes it isn't to my advantage being the pastor's wife.

The people in our church didn't know my story. When he told me his plan, I cried and covered my face. "I hate you for making me do this!"

"I know you do. I am not making you do this though. I just want you to be healed forever," Dallas explained.

I lashed out, "Right now, YOU are the only person I need to forgive!"

I thought about each person in the class and tried to gauge what their reaction would be when they found out that their pastor's wife had gone through with an abortion. The majority of my guesses proved to be accurate. There was one couple, however, with which I dreaded having to share my testimony. They were a younger couple and had lived a modest life. So you can only imagine the joy that leaped in my heart when I found out that this couple had opted out of the class. Whew! Off the hook. I could handle telling the others.

I only "thought" I was off the hook. That was not the case. After we were done with the forgiveness study, the Lord kept tugging on my heart, "You need to go tell this woman your story." Of course the woman He was refer- ring to was the one who had not participated in the class. I fought it. I tried to ignore it. God would not leave me alone though. I mustered up the courage to call her. We made some small talk and then I just laid it on the line.

"There is something I have to tell you," I said. I proceeded to tell to her all of the steps leading up to this phone call. I told her the only reason that I could think of that the Lord wanted me telling her was that I knew she had nieces that were of college age and may one day be faced with this decision. I encouraged her that if she ever needed to point someone in my direction, I would be happy to talk to them. She was very gracious while listening to my story and I was thankful that it was behind me.

I don't think a month went by when this woman called me and eagerly voiced, "I just want to thank you for your obedience to God the day that you called me. My niece called me and is worried that she might be pregnant and brought up the topic of abortion. If she is pregnant, will you talk to her?"

The answer, of course, was yes. It made me feel good that I had followed through with that task. It was a folder that I didn't have to stick in the Regret File in the cabinet of my mind. It gave me the courage to be more open and know that I could make a difference.

One regret that I have to live with is the fact that I had not told any of my kids and friends about my experience. I never realized the impact of that decision until the day that a very special friend of mine called to tell me that she had undergone an abortion. My heart broke. I felt I could have prevented it. I ached inside because I knew the torment and pain in store for her.

I didn't turn away from God, but I think by not letting Him heal me right away, it has hindered my Christian walk. Since making the decision to take care of the issue, I have felt closer to God than ever before. He has a plan for me. He has shown me I have a reason to live, not just exist.

He has given me strength and understanding. I lack nothing with Him.

In my healing I vowed that I would use this experience to help others based on 2 Corinthians 1:3-4.

2 Corinthians 1:3-4.
Praise be to the God and Father of our Lord Jesus Christ, the Father of compassion and the God of all comfort, who comforts us in all our troubles, so that we can comfort those in any trouble with the comfort we ourselves receive from God.

After reading Psalm 22, I realized that God had been my God from my mother's womb so I WILL declare His name to ALL the ends of the earth. I WILL turn to the Lord.

There are many ways people deal with this situation, but there is only one healthy way and that is Jesus Christ. He is my refuge and I hide under His wings. He is my Revealer of Truth. He is the Heart Healer. He is my Change Agent. He is the Lifter of my head. We have to go to Him and allow Him to be in control of the healing process.

1 Timothy 1:15
Here is a trustworthy saying that deserves full acceptance: Christ Jesus came into the world to save sinners —of whom I am the worst.

I do feel like the worst of sinners, but I know that I am growing in my Christian walk. I am praying and doing things for God twice as much as I used to but still only half as much as I should. The key, though, is that I am moving forward. I may still have setbacks and my emotions may overwhelm me at times, but I am getting up quicker now and dusting myself off and pressing forward. I also no longer consider September to be cursed. In fact, God has supplied that month with many blessings to assist me in turning my thought pattern around and give glory to Him.

God has blessed Dallas and I with five sons and two daughters and five grandchildren. He has entrusted me with many children in different ministry settings with which I have been able to build relationships. I am over-whelmed with the opportunities the Lord has given me to love His children and teach them about His Holy Word.

One of the exercises we had to do in the Healing Hearts class was to write our own Psalm. I am going to share mine with you and encourage you to review some of the Psalms in the Bible and then try it yourself. I found it very cleansing to be able to get my emotions, fears and hopes onto paper.

Oh God, hear me when I cry out! You are the Creator of all things. You promise peace and rest to Your children. I need the peace that only You can offer, Father!.

I know that You don't leave me, but, at times, I feel the need to cry loudly because I have gotten too far away from You. Can You hear me God?

My sin weighs me down. It's too heavy, Father! Please take it from me. I can't go another step. I can't move on until You lift it from me. Forgive me for sinning against You. Forgive me for taking the life of Your precious child.

I so desperately desire to do Your will. Why do I make it so difficult? Get me out of myself so I can clearly focus on You and understand what Your will is for me. Cleanse my heart Father. My heart is so black that no light can shine through until You make it clean.

My desire is to glorify You. Keep me focused. I don't want to lose sight of You, Abba Father. Your sweet, tender, healing hands rest upon my heart and mind. I don't deserve Your mercy or compassion.
   Hallelujah! You fill me up! Abba, my trust is in You. I want to hide IN You not hide FROM You. You have lifted my head. You have looked me in the eye and expressed Your awesome love to me through Your forgiveness and deliverance. I don't have to cry out now, Father, because You're close enough to hear my whispering voice. I am engulfed in Your presence. Your will be done in my life, Abba, Father.

   Psalm 51 was one that really touched my heart. It states that my sin is always before me. I could very much relate to David, the author of this Psalm. I wanted nothing more than for my sin to be blotted out and erased.
   I knew God to be a just God and I knew what I deserved. I so badly wanted to be cleansed and have the joy of my salvation restored.
   When penning this book, my heart related to verse `13 where it states, "Then I will teach transgressors Your ways, so that sinners will turn back to You." I want others to know that we don't have to hide in our shame forever. I want their hope and joy restored as well. When we come to God with a broken and contrite heart and we are willing to let Him put the pieces of our lives back together, THEN the peace will be restored and our hearts made clean.

Psalm 51:1-17
   1 Have mercy on me, O God, according to your unfailing love; according to your great compassion blot out my transgressions. 2 Wash away all my iniquity and

cleanse me from my sin. 3 For I know my transgressions, and my sin is always before me. 4 Against you, you only, have I sinned and done what is evil in your sight, so that you are proved right when you speak and justified when you judge. 5 Surely I was sinful at birth, sinful from the time my mother conceived me. 6 Surely you desire truth in the inner parts; you teach me wisdom in the inmost place. 7 Cleanse me with hyssop, and I will be clean; wash me, and I will be whiter than snow. 8 Let me hear joy and gladness; let the bones you have crushed rejoice. 9 Hide your face from my sins and blot out all my iniquity. 10 Create in me a pure heart, O God, and renew a steadfast spirit within me. 11 Do not cast me from your presence or take your Holy Spirit from me. 12 Restore to me the joy of your salvation and grant me a willing spirit, to sustain me. 13 Then I will teach transgressors your ways, and sinners will turn back to you. 14 Save me from bloodguilt, O God, the God who saves me, and my tongue will sing of your righteousness. 15 O Lord, open my lips, and my mouth will declare your praise. 16 You do not delight in sacrifice, or I would bring it; you do not take pleasure in burnt offerings. 17 The sacrifices of God are a broken spirit; a broken and contrite heart, O God, you will not despise.

11

THE ATTITUDE OF FORGIVENESS

If what I have described thus far in this book is something that you have not been through, you might have a hard time having any compassion on these men and women at all. You might feel that they deserve the mental anguish they are suffering. Be careful. There are no degrees of sin.

For what have you been forgiven? Don't forget that you have been saved with the same grace as these parents. We are all sinners.

These men and women know full well that what they did was wrong and they have to face that every day. Statistics reveal this. When you have 98% of the post-abortive women living in regret, it indicates they understand what they have done. It also shows that 98% of the women who have aborted, if given the chance to relive that moment, would do it differently.

Post-abortive men and women need to understand that in order to have their chains fall off, the truth of the situation must be faced, but not only that truth. They must face the truth that their sins have been forgiven by a God Who loves them so much He was willing to die on a cross for them. That is truth. That is freedom.

Psalm 107: 12-16
[12] So he subjected them to bitter labor; they stumbled, and there was no one to help. [13] Then they cried to the LORD in their trouble, and he saved them from their distress.[14] He brought them out of darkness, the utter darkness, and broke away their chains.[15] Let them give thanks to the LORD for his unfailing love and his wonderful deeds for mankind,[16] for he breaks down gates of bronze and cuts through bars of iron.

Forgiveness is a must. Through the healing process, post-abortive men and women are learning to forgive themselves, which can be a struggle in itself. They are also learning to forgive others that were involved in the situation.

Forgiveness may also need to take place for those on the outside looking in. Martin Luther King, Jr. said it best: "Forgiveness is not an occasional act, it is a constant attitude."

Of course abortion is a terrible thing. Of course, it goes against God's Word. However, judgment needs to be set aside. We don't see the whole picture, but God does. In that big picture, is God going to see us shunning these men and women who are wanting to be healed and searching for comfort or will He see us reaching out to them and leading them to where the Living Water is stored? We need to remember that God created each of these men and women also and they are precious in His sight.

Forgiveness is a matter of obedience. One definition of the word **forgive** that I found states that it means to cease to feel resentment towards. If we harbor resentment and bitterness against a brother and claim to have a great relationship with God then we are lying to ourselves.

We talk a lot in our church about having a rich relationship with God and a rich relationship with others. We cannot have one without the other. When we are struggling with our relationships with others, generally our relationship with God is not on the up and up. Forgiveness is hard because it doesn't seem "fair".

It is important to support these men and women who are trying to shake loose of their past and focus their eyes on the road ahead. We need to remind ourselves of how many things for which we have been forgiven. It will make the offenses of others look rather petty.

The longer we live in unforgiveness, the deeper that root of bitterness can grow. The deeper that it embeds itself; the harder it is to pull out. There will never be any peace in your life because you will be too busy keeping a record of wrongs of others. That is exhausting. The following verses of promises and instruction help us to understand the attitude we should have towards others whose sins we feel are bigger than ours.

Psalm 103:12

As far as the east is from the west, so far has he removed our transgressions from us.

Hebrews 8:12
For I will forgive their wickedness and will remember their sins no more.

Luke 6:38
Be merciful, just as your Father is merciful.

Luke 6:37
Do not judge, and you will not be judged. Do not condemn, and you will not be condemned. Forgive, and you will be forgiven.

Ephesians 4:31-32
Get rid of all bitterness, rage and anger, brawling and slander, along with every form of malice. Be kind and compassionate to one another, forgiving each other, just as in Christ God forgave you.

Acts 13:38
Therefore my brothers I want you to know that through Jesus the forgiveness of sins is proclaimed to you.

Romans 8:1
Therefore, there is now no condemnation for those who are in Christ Jesus,

Matthew 6:14-15
For if you forgive other people when they sin against you, your heavenly Father will also forgive you. But if you do not forgive others their sins, your Father will not forgive your sins.

Isaiah 55:7
Let the wicked forsake their ways and the unrighteous their thoughts. Let them turn to the LORD, and he will have mercy on them, and to our God, for he will freely pardon.

1 John 1:9
If we confess our sins, he is faithful and just and will forgive us our sins and purify us from all unrighteousness.

Understanding God's righteousness gives us a right understanding of ourselves and the need we have for a savior.

Jesus is the only way to freedom from this bondage. He is the only One who can break the bars of our yoke. He is the only One who can restore the peace in our minds and take the guilt and shame away. Everyone needs to know this.

If you are in bondage of any kind, if you suffer from guilt and shame and you have not asked Jesus into your heart yet, please take a moment right now and do this. You will not find the answers in drugs or alcohol. Although it may dull the pain for a while it will return upon sobering. Jesus can truly heal your heart, soul and mind.

Facing the reality of abortion will bring up many emotions. The men and women will deal with anger at the other person or people involved in the pregnancy situation. They will have to learn how to forgive these people.

When someone experiences depression, it is important to ask for help. Christians may have a hard time with this because they don't want people to think they are lacking in faith. We need to be perceptive to the signs of depression.

We hear a lot of stories on the news today of people reaching their breaking points through acts of violence and suicide and everybody that knew the person seems so surprised that this person was capable of it. Again, are we so wrapped up in our own lives that we don't take the time to get out of ourselves? Are we not wanting our lives interrupted so therefore don't take the time to look into someone else's eyes and see what people are dealing with?

Psalm 34:17-18
The righteous cry out, and the LORD hears them; he delivers them from all their troubles. The LORD is close to the brokenhearted and saves those who are crushed in spirit.

Psalm 107:19-20
Then they cried to the LORD in their trouble, and he saved them from their distress. He sent out his Word and healed them; he rescued them from the grave.

Prayer for post-abortive men and women is crucial. Pray for their courage to face the truth and their desire to understand the truth. One of the first things they need to comprehend is found in Psalm 139; knowing Who they belong to and how He created them.

Psalm 139:13-16
[13] For you created my inmost being; you knit me together in my mother's womb. [14] I praise you because I am fearfully and wonderfully made; your works are wonderful, I know that full well. [15] My frame was not hidden from you when I was made in the secret place, when I was woven together in the depths of the earth. [16] Your

eyes saw my unformed body; all the days ordained for me were written in your book before one of them came to be.

Grieving is an important factor in any healing. Although a post-abortive man or woman may feel that they don't have the right to grieve, they must find a way. Just because that baby is no longer inside of its mother, the memory of that child is forever embedded in the mother's and father's mind. They already realize their part in the sin of the abortion so they must show their grief to reveal their hearts in the repentance of that sin. Grief for their child is also important. It is a loss. Parents mourn the loss of their children.

It is also essential for the man or woman to find a safe place to express their feelings of grief, whether it is a close friend, a pastor or a support group. There are many websites and classes that are thoroughly equipped to help men and women through this healing process.

12

IN CONCLUSION

As a nation we need to mourn for these children because they are no more. However, the mothers and fathers of these children are still here and they need healing.

As I mentioned before, I worry when women say it doesn't bother them after having had an abortion because usually their attitudes and actions say something completely different. We need to watch for self-medication through drugs and alcohol. Watch for eating disorders. These men and women that struggle with depression or become withdrawn may not even realize it at the time that it is directly related to the abortion.

They might not link those behaviors with their past, but it will catch up with them and that's who I weep for. The devil, of course, can help with the deception just like he did Eve in the garden by planting seeds of doubt and by twisting words. He will help us justify it for as long as he can get by with it by telling us that what is inside of us are just products of conception, not a literal life knit into us by God.

I rationalized my abortion by thinking it was the ON-LY WAY to keep my spouse and the ONLY WAY to escape shame. The truth was the ONLY WAY to heal was to turn to Jesus. If these men and women try to deal with it any other way they will live in continual chains.

Even though we have to suffer natural consequences for our sin, God still loves us and will provide for us like He provided clothes for Adam and Eve before driving them out of the garden. These men and women will try to hide just like Adam and Eve did also, in shame, never volunteering information.

Matthew 11:28-29
Come to me, all you who are weary and burdened, and I will give you rest. Take my yoke upon you and learn from me, for I am gentle and humble in heart, and you will find rest for your souls.

Thank you for letting me trust you with my story. It took me a long time to finish this as I would go through moments of panic. I was terrified to reveal my past to people, especially those who have known me but may not have known my history.

God's voice would come through so loud and clear to me though, "You are going to change lives; you are going to save lives through your story." There were many other writing projects I wanted to do but God would whisper, "I know you want to do those, but this is the one that I NEED you to do not only for the sake of others but for your own sake, to continue your healing process." I know that I will be able to do my other projects, but I really believe that until I obeyed and did this one that I would not be able to really rest.

My prayer is that men and women who have experienced the horror of abortion will read this book and see that they are not alone. I pray they can understand that it is possible to live a life without condemnation. I don't promise that their memories will fade but I do promise that they will be filled with the hope of reuniting with their child one day. My hope is that they will be able to gain the confidence and the boldness to speak up and tell their own stories so that even more lives can be saved.

For those who pick up this book and have not been through this act, my hope is that it will be a tool in your toolbox to be able to reach out and help someone you may know who is struggling with this very thing. I hope that my words, my research and my story will give you a better understanding of the world in which these parents live. May your heart be one of greater compassion. May you seek to bring healing into their lives and not judgment. You have an opportunity to see lives be healed and changed if you know what they are dealing with and can reach out and share love and acceptance. Gently lead them to the foot of the cross of Jesus Christ where sins are washed away.

MY PSALM

_____

_____

_____

_____

_____

_____

_____

_____

_____

_____

_____

_____

_____

_____

_____

_____

_____

_____

_____

_____

_____

_____

I FORGIVE YOU

MY TESTIMONY

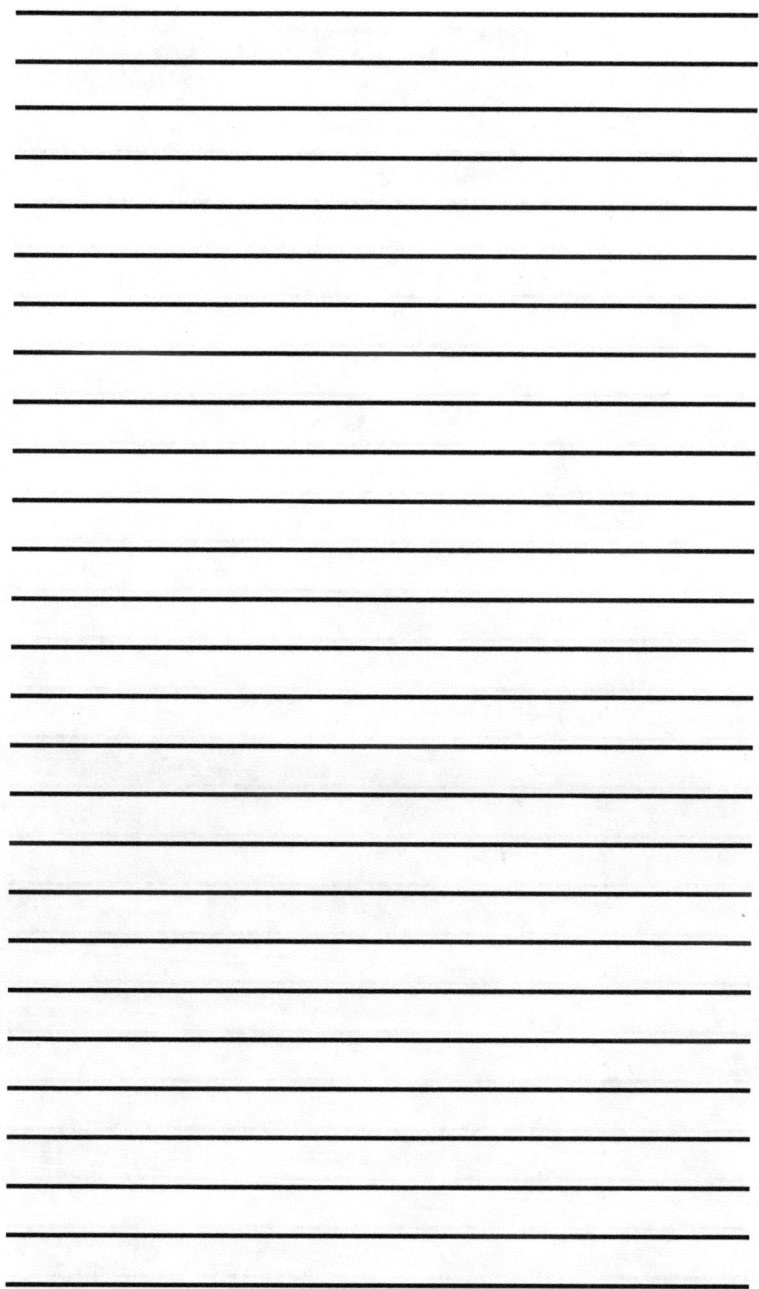

BIBLE VERSES

_____

_____

_____

_____

_____

_____

_____

_____

_____

_____

_____

_____

_____

_____

_____

_____

_____

_____

_____

_____

_____

MY LIFE VERSE

_____

_____

_____

_____

_____

_____

_____

_____

WHY I CHOSE THIS VERSE

_____

_____

_____

_____

_____

_____

_____

_____

_____

_____

_____

SYMPTOMS OF

POST ABORTION SYNDROME

1. The inability to process the painful thoughts and emotions, especially guilt, anger, and grief, that arise from one or more unplanned pregnancies and abortions.
2. The inability to identify the loss that has been experienced
3. The inability to come to peace with God, oneself, and others involved in the pregnancy and abortion decision.
4. Guilt
5. Anxiety
6. Avoidance behaviors
7. Psychological numbing
8. Depression
9. Re-experiencing events related to the abortion
10. Preoccupation with becoming pregnant again, anxiety over fertility and childbearing issues
11. Interruption or disruption of the bonding with present or future children
12. Self-abuse/self-destructive behaviors
13. Anniversary reactions
14. Brief psychotic disorder.

Romans Road to Salvation

1.The reason everyone needs salvation is because we have all sinned.

Romans 3:10-12
As it is written: There is no one righteous, not even one; there is no one who understands; there is no one who seeks God. All have turned away, they have together become worthless; there is no one who does good, not even one.

Romans 3:23
for all have sinned and fall short of the glory of God,

2. The consequence of sin is death.

Romans 6:23
For the wages of sin is death, but the gift of God is eternal life in Christ Jesus our Lord.

3. Jesus Christ paid the price for our sins.

Romans 5:8
But God demonstrates his own love for us in this: While we were still sinners, Christ died for us.

4. We receive salvation and eternal life through faith in Jesus Christ.

Romans 10:9-13
If you declare with your mouth, "Jesus is Lord," and believe in your heart that God raised him from the dead, you will be saved. For it is with your heart that you believe and are justified, and it is with your mouth that you profess your faith and are saved. As Scripture says, "Anyone who

believes in him will never be put to shame. "For there is no difference between Jew and Gentile—the same Lord is Lord of all and richly blesses all who call on him, for, "Everyone who calls on the name of the Lord will be saved."

5. Salvation through Jesus Christ brings us into a relationship of peace with God.

Romans 5:1
Therefore, since we have been justified through faith, we have peace with God through our Lord Jesus Christ,.

Romans 8:1
Therefore, since we have been justified through faith, we have peace with God through our Lord Jesus Christ

Romans 8:38
For I am convinced that neither death nor life, neither angels nor demons, neither the present nor the future, nor any powers, [39] neither height nor depth, nor anything else in all creation, will be able to separate us from the love of God that is in Christ Jesus our Lord.

Responding to the Romans Road

1. Admit you are a sinner and understand that as a sinner, you deserve death.
2. Believe Jesus Christ died on the cross to save you from your sin and death.
3. Repent by turning from your old life of sin to a new life in Christ.
4. Receive, through faith in Jesus Christ, His free gift of salvation. It can be yours today!

Programs to Assist in the Healing of Post-Abortive Men and Women

Project Rachel and Project Joseph

Lumina/Hope and Healing

Rachel's Vineyard

PACE Programs

Healing Hearts International Ministries – Binding Up the Broken Hearted Study for women and Wounded Warrior Study for men

Silent No More

Abortion Recovery CARE Line at:

1.866.4.My.Recovery

BIBLIOGRAPHY

Berne, Emma Carlson (Editor). Abortion. 120 pages. Detroit, Thomson/Gale. 2007

Farlex. "The Free Dictionary/Thesaurus". 2013. http://www.thefreedictionary.com

Ashley, Scott. "How Does the Bible Define Sin". Good News Magazine. April 1997. http://www.ucg.org/christian-living/how-does-bible-define-sin/

The Center for Bio-Ethical Reform. "Abortion Facts". Abortion-No.org 2005 http://www.abortionno.org/abortion-facts/

Elliot Institute. "Abortion Risks: A list of major physical complications related to abortion". AfterAbortion.org. November 1999. http://afterabortion.org/1999/abortion-risks-a-list-of-major-physical-complications-related-to-abortion/

Clinger, Matt. "The curse of Adam's silence - a MAN's post-abortion testimony". January 20, 2012. LifeSiteNews.com. http://www.lifesitenews.com/news/the-curse-of-adams-silence-a-mans-post-abortion-testimony/

"Post Abortion Help". September 21, 2013. Operation Rescue. http://www.operationrescue.org/about-abortion/post-abortion-help/

"Post Abortion Syndrome" 2013. Embracing Options. http://www.hisbranches.org/eo/ops/pace.htm

Liljenberg, Gary and Sue. "Healing Hearts Ministries". 1988. http://www.healinghearts.org/about.php

Fairchild, Mary. "What is Romans Road". 2013. About.com. http://christianity.about.com/od/conversion/qt/romansroad.htm

"United States Abortion Statistics". 2012. Minnesota Citizens Concern for Life. http://www.mccl.org/us-abortion-stats.html

Joseph, Frank. "The Abortion-Breast Cancer Link is America's Best Kept Secret". April 7, 2012. Abortion Breast Cancer Link. http://www.errantskeptics.org/Abortion-Breast-Cancer.htm

Gold, Rachel Benson. "Lessons From Before Roe: Will Past Be Prologue". March 2003 Volume 6, Number 1. GuttmacherInstitute. http://www.guttmacher.org/pubs/tgr/06/1/gr060108.html

"When Can I Hear My Baby's Heartbeat?". April 2012. Bbycenter.expertadvice. http://www.babycenter.com/404_when-can-i-hear-my-babys-heartbeat_10349811.bc

"What is Anorexia Nervosa? What is Bulimia Nervosa?". August 21, 2013. Medical News Today. http://www.medicalnewstoday.com/articles/105102.php

ABOUT THE AUTHOR

JoEllen Claypool is the author of A Realist's Guide to Being a Pastor's Wife, Realistic Tips to Being a Pastor's Wife and a contributing author of An Eclectic Collage Volume 2: Relationships of Life. She serves in the ministry with her husband who pastors a small country church in Caldwell, Idaho. Together, they enjoy homeschooling their two youngest of seven children. Understanding the impact that one person can make, JoEllen is eager to reach out and encourage others to make right choices so that lives can be saved.

www.ingramcontent.com/pod-product-compliance
Lightning Source LLC
Chambersburg PA
CBHW060811050426
42449CB00008B/1635